About the Author

Stuart McKibbin has been working in the creative side of direct marketing for over 40 years, many of them as Head of Copy at *Reader's Digest*. He has helped to promote successfully a variety of services and products, including magazines, books, videos, holidays, language courses, roses, wines, toys, collectibles, banking, paintings and mobile telephones. He was described by *Interactive Marketing* as "one of the outstanding wordsmiths of the last 30 years" and by the Marketing Director at *Reader's Digest* as "one of the legends of the promotion copywriting world".

Stuart has contributed articles to *Punch*, *The Guardian* and *Campaign* and is the author of a satirical book called *A Cynic's Guide to Management*.

GW00708681

THE BUSINESS OF PERSUASION

Copywriting Skills and Techniques that Get Results!

Stuart McKibbin

Oak Tree Press

Dublin

Oak Tree Press
Merrion Building
Lower Merrion Street
Dublin 2, Ireland
http://www.oaktreepress.com

© 2000 Stuart McKibbin

A catalogue record of this book is
available from the British Library.

ISBN 1 86076 175-5

Printed in the Republic of Ireland by Colour Books Ltd.

Contents

Preface

This is a book about the methods, techniques and tricks of the trade of writing what is known as "direct response" copy — a genre that embraces not only direct mail and mail order but also, increasingly, the electronic media ... television, radio, the telephone and now of course the Internet.

The objective of securing an immediate response from the consumer, in the form of an order, a request for further information, a personal quotation, a payment or a gift not only helps to concentrate the copywriter's mind; it also imposes a strict and salutary discipline on "creativity" and helps to eliminate creative self-indulgence — those wild and wacky flights of fevered fancy that seem to have an irresistible appeal to the poets manqués, aspiring playwrights and unpublished novelists who have been responsible for so much ineffective, self-indulgent and down-right irritating advertising. Egregious examples of their work are proudly exhibited every year at festivals and award ceremonies held in the world's glossier watering holes, where advertising people forgather for mutual ego-massage and to award putty statuettes and medals to each other.

In stark contrast, direct response writers judge each other's efforts by the unforgiving test of *results* — not aesthetic judgement or finer feelings, but precisely measurable response. If these are what interest you, *The Business of Persuasion* has much to offer you.

Obviously the book, being written in English, is aimed primarily at those who promote their services or products in the language — a category that embraces many more than the Anglo-phone countries. Since English has become a commercial lingua franca, it is now the language in which Koreans sell to Germans, Finns to Spaniards and of course the UK and US to everyone. Not only will the book be of value to all who use the English language to promote their products; the creative principles that it explains are equally applicable in any other language.

Finally, the book contains important lessons for a whole new generation of direct marketers whose focus is on the possibilities of the new electronic age. Mike Moran, Commercial Director of Toyota (GB), recently wrote in an article: "Is it just me, or is most dotcom advertising utter drivel?" He went on to say, "The Internet may be a brave new world for dotcom marketers, but they would do well to look to their more experienced forefathers for help with their communication strategies."

The following pages distil the experience of one such forefather and reveal what he has learned in the course of a working lifetime engaged in the demanding, challenging — but potentially hugely rewarding and satisfying — business of persuasion.

Chapter 1

Understanding Motivations

Before you write a word of copy you need to have in mind a clear picture of the motives that anyone might have for buying a product or service of the kind you hope to sell. People buy things for a variety of different reasons. These range from emotional and aesthetic to hard-nosed practical and financial reasons. Sometimes a purchase is made for more than one reason, some weighing more heavily than others in the buyer's estimation. To be in a position to persuade anyone to buy what you are selling you need to have in your own mind a clear picture of all the main reasons why anyone might wish to have a product of this kind — the benefits to which it provides a key, the uses to which it can be put, the hopes and ambitions that it holds out a realistic prospect of being able to help a purchaser to realise. Once you understand the range of benefits to which your product opens doors, you can move on to the next stage, which is to find some way to dramatise them convincingly. With some products this is easy. With others — more versatile or complex ones — it can be a great help to sit down and draw up an analysis of motivation.

Here, for example, is a breakdown of all the motives there could be for buying a do-it-yourself book whose contents are designed to help readers to carry out their own repair jobs around the home and garden:

General Motivation: Reasons for Wanting Things Repaired

- To save the cost of replacement.

- To regain the use of something that's not working.

- To save from the scrap-heap some object for which you have an affection.

- To remove a potential source of danger.

- Prompt action can prove less costly than delaying a repair.

- Something that needs mending is a source of mute reproach.

- Home-improvement: add to the value of property and make a home more comfortable.

Specific Motivation: Reasons for Wanting to do the Job Yourself

- To save the cost of professional work.

- To save time; you don't want to wait for assistance.

- It can't wait (you can hear the sound of dripping water *now*).

- There's no other way to get the job done. Where can you take a piece of broken china to be mended — or an electronic clock?

- Satisfaction — first, independence; and, second, the sense of fulfilment that self-reliance provides.

- Admiration: "Darling, you're wonderful"; "Gosh Dad, thanks a lot!"

So far, the results of your analysis could probably be used to sell any product of this kind. What you now need to do is to distinguish the product you are selling from others on the market, to demonstrate all the features that make it superior to them, including (where applicable) the terms on which it is available. Your task is to match the features of your product to the range of purposes for which a purchaser might use it in order to reach realistic goals. And to highlight any other attractive features of your offer.

What's Special about this Book

- Step-by-step instructions
- Clear illustrations
- Range of jobs covered
- Publisher's reputation

What's Special about the Offer

- Chance to win in a sweepstakes or contest
- A premium (free gift) for prompt order
- Free approval
- Option of paying by instalments.

Having analysed features of the product and offer that could motivate people to buy it, you can move on to present these features to the reader in a striking, appealing and convincing way. For example, the front cover of a brochure describing the book might feature photographs that illustrate a variety of people in a range of situations involving a repair, each with a caption that highlights a benefit of having the book: SAVE TIME, SAVE MONEY, SAVE PRIZED POSSESSIONS FROM THE SCRAP-HEAP — and so on.

The point about saving money could be rammed home elsewhere in the brochure by including a table that compares some typical tradesmen's charges for repairs with the much-smaller price of a book that shows readers how to do the job themselves for no more than the cost of any raw materials required. You might also show one or two typical pages from the book in order to demonstrate to readers how clear and easy to follow are the instructions that the book provides.

Your Motivation Analysis doesn't have to be so formal or elaborate. Let's look now at the field of insurance — first of all, of household contents. Why might people want it?

Here are the main reasons:

- Perception of the growing risk of being burgled.

- Risks of damage caused by natural disasters — storm, flood, etc — fuelled by media coverage of hurricanes and floods.

- Rising costs of replacing possessions that are lost, damaged or destroyed

- In the case of antiques, jewellery, etc stolen, lost or damaged, the consequent financial loss can be substantial.

Now health insurance:

- ***Immediacy***: Patients treated privately can by-pass health plan waiting lists.

- ***Comfort***: A private room in hospital provides a higher degree of comfort than a public ward, with such amenities as an en suite bathroom, etc.

- ***Privacy and Convenience***: Occupants of private rooms find it easier to keep in touch with family, friends and business with such amenities as bedside telephone, unrestricted visiting, etc.

- ***Choice***: Patients who are treated privately have a choice of specialist and hospital. They can also choose when to have the treatment if it doesn't happen to be urgent.

- ***Cost***: The increasing cost of medical and surgical treatment, drugs, investigative procedures and hospital accommodation combine to make it difficult, if not impossible, for most patients to fund private treatment from their own resources. Insurance provides a realistic way of making it affordable.

- ***Responsibility***. As well as concern for care, people with families naturally want tł dependants.

Having assembled such a list of reasons why anyon to buy this kind of insurance (*Generic Motivation*) yo ...ove on next to what I call *Specific Motivation* — by which I mean features of this product that make it arguably superior to others of its kind. For example:

- Wider cover

- Fewer exclusions

- Lower premium

- Smaller excess (the proportion of any claim that the policy-holder has to pay)

- Insurer's track record

- Size of insurer's resources

- Handles claims swiftly and sympathetically

- Keeps paperwork to a minimum

- Has user-friendly claim forms

- Issues policies which explain in easy-to-understand language precisely what cover is provided and what the exclusions are.

Finally, you can turn to salient features of the offer and any competitive advantages provided. For example:

- Discount

- Premium

- Chance to win in a contest or sweepstakes

- Exclusivity

- Limited availability

Deadline for eligibility.

Charities

The motivations for giving to charity are different, but they are there all the same and include:

- *Sympathy* — a genuine, spontaneous reaction to the suffering of others, which generates a desire to help.

- *Compassion* — the fellow-feeling of those who have first-hand experience of the kind of suffering, problem or deprivation which the charity exists to help.

- *Guilt* — of the kind that people often feel about the contrast between their own comfortable circumstances and the sufferings of others.

- *Gratitude* — gifts are often made to charity as a kind of thanks offering — either for the donor's own good fortune, or for help received in time of need from the charity concerned.

- *Self-interest* — as, for example, in the case of charities which fund medical research of which one day donors themselves, or members of their families, could be beneficiaries.

- *Anger* — a sense of outrage at the spectacle of suffering or deprivation.

The most significant differences between some products are the advertisements for them. And in the case of products marketed direct to the consumer, the biggest differences between many of them are found in the copy that is written to promote them. If you can succeed in linking your product with some strong emotion or desire you are well on the way to making a sale. Only rarely will features that are intrinsic to the product provide the strongest impulse to buy it. More often, it is the close link that your copy supplies between the product and some widely-shared desire that is the crucial factor in making a sale. This is another reason why it pays to analyse the product or service that you have to sell, and identify every possible reason why anyone might benefit from buying it.

Take, as another example, membership of a motoring organisation — which is essentially the right to call on various services that the organisation can offer. Why might anyone consider joining? Here are the main reasons:

- *Convenience* — Having a car break down on the road is frustrating and inconvenient. Inability to complete your journey is at the very least a cause of irritation. If the breakdown causes you to miss a business appointment there could be a financial penalty. And — depending where the car breaks down — inability to move it could prove embarrassing.

- *Fear* — Being marooned on a deserted road — especially at night — can be a frightening experience, particularly for a woman travelling alone.

- *Representation* — The organisation might be said to represent the interests of motorists, giving them a voice. Because it speaks for so many of them its voice and views command respect.

- *Service* — Members can make use of a range of services to motorists, e.g. advice on the best buys in car insurance and on legal problems, route recommendations, etc. All these are of course in addition to breakdown services, and possibly — if the car cannot be repaired on the spot — onward transportation to the driver's destination.

Having identified all the reasons why someone might consider joining a motoring organisation, the writer needs to go on and establish why it should be the one for which he is writing a recruitment mailing, by drawing attention to the strength of its competitive position. He might, for example, point out that its breakdown service is available nation-wide, round the clock, throughout the year. He can point to the size of its workforce, the number of patrols on call, the comprehensiveness of their equipment and the thorough nature of their training.

Once having established the strength of its competitive position, the writer can turn without embarrassment to the cost of membership. When quoting a price it is often helpful to *belittle* it. This might be done by comparing it with either or both of two alternatives. The first (if of course the comparison is favourable) is the cost of joining this organisation rather than one of its rivals. The second comparison would be with the daunting costs of not being able to use the breakdown service — among them the charge for a tow or transport to the nearest garage.

By analysing in this way both the product and the reasons why people might want it, it is possible to construct a convincing case for buying it — converting a relatively humdrum concept into an appealing proposition.

Having identified the reasons for wanting a product or service, it is then necessary to focus on your particular item, i.e. features intrinsic to that product and the organisation that makes or offers it — in other words, competitive advantages.

If, for example, you are selling an insecticide, does it kill a wider than usual spectrum of pests? Is it *organic* — a natural product, free from toxic chemicals? Is it safe to apply in gardens used by pets and children? Is it made by a firm whose reputation stands particularly high in this field?

Is the car that you are selling cheaper to service than the model it replaces? Is the recommended interval between services significantly longer? Does the manufacturer offer some unusual form of guarantee?

Some of the selling copy written for the product should focus sharply on features of it that yield an arguable competitive advantage.

More than half the battle in clinching a sale is to find some strong motive for buying that kind of product — and a striking way to associate your product with it. If you can do this successfully it becomes much easier to clinch a sale by describing in detail all the features of your product that make it superior to rivals.

But I will only want to buy your product, instead of someone else's, if I have first been persuaded that I really need this kind of article. Only then will I be interested in comparing the relative merits of the various products of this genre. To take the example of the health book, mentioned in the next chapter, I am likely to feel that I can get along nicely without any of the titles on the market until one comes along that is presented to me in a different light as, for example, a "personal health service", or as "health insurance", or as a way to take advantage of the latest developments in preventive medicine.

Now that I am persuaded of this title's relevance, I am greatly prejudiced in its favour and consequently more receptive to a catalogue of all the features that make it so superior.

In other words, the fact that there are so many "me-too" products is no reason to try and sell them with me-too advertising!

Overcoming Obstacles

As well as a clear view of all the possible reasons why people might be persuaded to buy, it is useful to bear in mind reasons why they might *not* accept your offer. These cover a wide range, and not all of them relate directly to the nature of the product. Failure to accept your offer could be due to nothing more than lethargy or inertia. Hence the value of such devices for impelling readers to act immediately as premiums and prize schemes that incorporate a deadline. "Limited stocks" and "limited time" are two obvious reasons to offer in order to explain why prompt action is essential. Other impediments to instant acceptance of your offer may be more directly related to the nature of the product:

Cost

This is the commonest reason that people give themselves for not accepting an offer. This is why, when you reveal the price, it pays to do everything you can to diminish its size in the eyes of the reader. This is best done by comparison — comparison, not only with the price of competitive products, but also with alternatives to purchase. For example, the price of a practical handbook can be made to seem less daunting by comparing the cost of the book with that of professional help and advice in whatever field its contents cover. If it happens to be a do-it-yourself book you can legitimately compare its price with the cost of employing painters, carpenters and plasterers etc. If its subject is accountancy or health, the comparison might be with the fees that professionals charge for a few minutes of their time.

Complacency

A common reason for failing to accept some offers is complacency — a belief that "it couldn't happen to me". Burglaries, fires, floods and various other misfortunes are events — reported daily in the media — which many believe only affect other people. Because the news is entirely about other people, most of us tend to believe that we will never be caught up in the kind of events reported.

One way to overcome complacency is to bring home to the reader — without becoming too alarmist — the reality of risk. Here statistics can be helpful if they are presented skilfully. Thus, rather than tell the reader that "there are 60,000 hospital admissions every week", the point can be brought home more tactfully and readably by saying something like this:

"Every day, x thousand of us who consult the family doctor will be told that we need an operation."

"Every day, 6,000 motorists who leave home in the morning on their way to work, to the shops or to drop children off at school will be involved in a traffic accident; of these, no fewer than 2,000 will suffer the anxiety, pain and discomfort of personal injury as well as the cost and inconvenience of damage to their cars."

Rather than setting out to frighten the reader too directly, it is better to take the line that facts speak for themselves, and show that, while the worst may never happen, it is only sensible to take appropriate precautions.

Diffidence

Lack of confidence in their ability to take advantage of it can sometimes deter people from buying certain kinds of product — for example, a book on gardening, cookery or a do-it-yourself manual, a computer or a certain kind of tool. It is therefore prudent to write copy that convinces the reader that he has all it takes to make proper use of the product, or at least that any knowledge he may lack will be rapidly acquired by following the full, clear and easily-understood instructions that come with it.

Squeamishness

Some subjects are hard to contemplate with equanimity. The possibilities of injury or illness are not something that most of us wish to confront. Some people never make a will for no better reason than a superstitious feeling that facing up to the certainty of death is somehow likely to bring forward the event. Squeamishness and superstition are best overcome by taking a brisk, reassuring, reasonable line that conveys a message on these lines:

> "Look, we're both responsible, sensible people who want to look after ourselves and our dependants. Here is something that we all know we ought to do, and once you have done it, you'll be able to sit back with an easy mind."

Skilfully executed, the switch from "we" and "us" to "you" passes almost unnoticed!

Chapter 2

The Creative Process:
How to Find Ideas that Work

Having established in your mind a clear picture of possible motives for buying a product of this nature, as well as of the features that might persuade people to buy yours rather than a competitor's, you arrive at the next crucial step in the creative process. This is to find some striking, memorable way of presenting your product to the consumer.

This is a two-stage process: the first involves coming up with as many ways as you can think of to make all the points that you think might be helpful in persuading anyone to buy. Naturally these need to be made in a way that arrests attention without sacrificing credibility.

Subject as it is of much portentous, ill-informed discussion, the "creative process" — the thought processes by which good advertising ideas are produced — is difficult to pin down and describe. The process is a source of some despair to managements who tend to be irritated and frustrated by their inability to schedule, analyse or programme it, and in many cases even to recognise the genuine end product in the shape of a good creative idea. Attempts to explain it are made all the harder by the fact that there is no single way to go about it — no one "correct" approach. Creative individuals each evolve their own techniques.

Nevertheless the process of producing good ideas is so central to the subject of this book that I feel an attempt must be made to shed some light on it, and provide at least a few tips on how it can be approached.

Leaving aside the possibility, which is always there, of random inspiration — the sudden flash of inspiration which can instantly be recognised as a good idea — experience has taught that there are several ways in which the formulation of ideas can be purposefully approached and deliberately encouraged. And perhaps this can best be explained by way of actual examples.

Example

You have been retained to sell private health insurance. One of the principal benefits is that any treatment needed is received immediately — private patients do not have to take their turn on a long waiting list. The challenge is to dramatise this important benefit in some striking and memorable way.

One possible creative solution would lie along these lines. Anyone who has ever visited a hospital will have noticed a forest of signposts, each pointing to a different department of the hospital: "Pathology, X-ray, Paediatrics, Out-patients, In-patients, etc".

So what about a brochure whose cover features several of these signposts — including Out-patients and In-patients. Beside these is shown an arrow with the caption "This way for Impatients". The arrow points to a paragraph or two of copy which explains that those who are impatient to receive immediate treatment without the delays involved in having to join a waiting list can do so by taking out private health insurance.

Example

From the kind of insurance that pays for the cost of treatment in the event of falling ill, let's turn to another kind of health insurance — protection against getting ill. It is in this metaphorical sense that the concept of "health insurance" might be used to sell a book on healthy living — incorporating advice about such topics as exercise, smoking and diet.

There are hundreds of such publications on the market, and even the greatest health fanatic tends to flinch at the prospect of yet another book crammed with well-intentioned nagging about the desirability of drinking less and exercising more, not to mention eating fewer eggs and more green vegetables.

So instead of trying to sell yet another healthy-lifestyle book, might it not be smarter to sell it as "low-cost health insurance" — an important new "health service" from the publisher?

Once again, metaphor can be used to present a fairly commonplace, humdrum prospect in a new, more arresting perspective.

Example

You are writing an appeal designed to raise funds for a charity that aims to help the homeless.

Now homelessness is a somewhat abstract concept, and those who lack a home of their own are too often lumped together as an anonymous mass described as "the homeless". So the challenge is to find some way to confront the complacency of those who have a home, and persuade them to make a gift to help those who don't. One way to do this would be to build an appeal around the one thing that symbolises possession of a home — the key to its front door.

The copy would remind readers of their relative good fortune in having — in pocket or handbag — the means of gaining access at will to a home of their own. It would, of course, lead to the punchline:

> "It now lies within your power to help give to less fortunate people something infinitely precious that you are lucky enough to take for granted — the key to a home of your own."

Common to these examples is the use of a simple metaphor or symbol — ideally one that can be featured both in words and graphics — for the major benefit that you want to put across.

In one case the appeal is to self-interest (the assurance of prompt treatment) while in another the appeal is to compassion. The point I am trying to make is that whatever the nature of your proposition, it helps if you can find some memorable way to make it.

And, having assembled as many of these metaphors and symbols as possible, the next and final stage is to decide how — and in what sequence — to present them. Some may be better suited to presentation in a letter; others might be featured more effectively in a brochure. The "health insurance" concept for instance is essentially verbal, and is therefore probably less suitable for use in a brochure of which graphic illustration is an important component. And in the case of a book of this nature, a brochure would probably be needed in order to illustrate the range of subjects covered, the benefits offered to readers and their families and (in the form of specimen pages from the book) the clarity and visual appeal of the editorial treatment they receive. The health insurance metaphor might therefore be better reserved for the accompanying letter.

However, in the case of private health insurance, the idea of a signpost for "Impatients" could be used in either a letter or brochure. Which to go for (but you could of course choose to have both) depends on how many conceptual `building blocks" you have managed to assemble, and the number of them that call for graphic illustration.

The concept of the front door key in a charity appeal could again be used in either a letter or brochure. In the case of a charity, however, use of both letter and brochure might seem a touch extravagant. And when appealing for funds to help people in need it is important to avoid any appearance of extravagance.

Some of the larger, wealthier charities which can afford to test the component parts of their appeal packages have found that they not only save money by printing their letters and leaflets on paper of poor quality; the appearance of frugality this gives to their appeals also seems to be welcomed by supporters and produces both more and larger gifts.

To succeed in making a sale the copywriter has to find a way to penetrate the thick carapace of boredom and indifference developed by consumers to protect themselves against the barrage of advertising to which they are subjected. Far from being willing to give advertisers a hearing, most people are reluctant to read copy with any close attention. It is therefore salutary for copywriters to bear constantly in mind the fact that they have probably secured no more than a brief and tenuous hold on a small part of the reader's attention.

From this it follows that to get under the reader's skin and persuade him to look closely at your offer, you need to confront him with some striking proposition — and the way to do this is by enabling the consumer to see whatever you are selling — however commonplace it may be — in an arresting new perspective that bathes it in a striking and flattering light.

This is an objective more easily stated than achieved, but it is precisely in the achievement of this goal that the process of "creativity" resides. And there are one or two techniques that make the process easier.

The first is to present a familiar concept in a context that is dramatically *unfamiliar*. The well-known conventions of a prize draw provide two examples of this process. This one makes its point by mocking the tired clichés of a prize draw to hold out the prospect of "winning", not some desirable object, but a booby prize. The technique is used here to promote membership of a motoring organisation.

> Every day on Britain's roads, motorists take part in one of the great lotteries of our time. The "prizes" — all unwelcome and undesirable enough to merit the description "Booby Prizes" — are failure to start, or a breakdown — without having anyone to call on to get you out of trouble (such as the x thousand patrolmen that the AA has on the roads — all not only on the roads, but on the ball, and swiftly on the spot.

Every day there are something like x thousand "Booby Prizes" to be won. These range from a full scale major breakdown en route for a holiday — with a misery bonus if a car happens to be full of pets and children at the time ("Thousands of prizes simply must be won"!) — to the smaller but nevertheless unwelcome consolation prizes of a car's stubborn failure to start. Then of course there are all the mechanical failures caused by accidents.

To make sure of your chance to carry off one of these undesirable awards in the great Booby Prize Draw, just don't respond to this offer.

But if you are not tempted by the thought of picking up one of these prizes, and even less attracted by the thought of them going to your partner, just complete the application form below.

The second example again makes use of prize draw conventions to sell a product — magazine or book — that offers the reader financial advice, including advice on tax matters:

HOW YOU COULD WIN A SUBSTANTIAL PRIZE WITHOUT GAMBLING A PENNY!

This letter brings you chances to win substantial prizes without gambling a penny.

First the prizes you could win. Next to winning someone else's money, the nicest kind of prize is surely to win back from the Inland Revenue some of your own hard-earned income. That's the sort of cash prize you could win with (magazine).

And if you can't actually win a colour TV, a car, a washing machine, a holiday — or some other desirable piece of merchandise — it would be no small consolation to be able to buy one at a saving. That's the kind of consolation prize we offer you chances to win.

You could win any of these prizes without gambling a penny. Let me tell you how.

One way to enlist a reader's interest in the product is to highlight a number of relevant key words — and then go on to summarise in a sentence the product's obvious relevance. The sentence can either ask a question (obviously in a way which clearly implies that the product either is, or has, the answer); or, alternatively, it can make a statement which suggests what the product has to offer in this field.

JOGGING: Is It Really Safe?

Or

JOGGING: When It Isn't Safe

VITAMINS: Are You Getting Enough?

Or

VITAMINS: Your Daily Requirements Explained

In effect what you are doing is holding up a sequence of placards, each featuring a word or phrase that is likely to capture attention — and for each of them revealing at a glance the product's relevance. In this way it is possible to indicate a range of benefits without getting bogged down in too much explanatory detail. The device is particularly suited to a brochure, where a lot of ground can be covered in a way that doesn't use much space.

Where the need is to impart a lot of information you can do this in either (or both) of two ways. One is to ask questions in a way that suggests interesting answers; the other is to provide interesting information.

For example, beneath the headline "DO YOU KNOW . . .?" you might ask a question: "How Often Men Should Have Sex?"

And beside the headline "DID YOU KNOW . . . ?" there would be a revelation: "The biggest health risk for young men is having sex too often; while for older men it is not having sex often enough!"

The product itself can often be a source of good ideas. A talk with the various people involved in its sale and manufacture can easily spark ideas. This example illustrates the process — central to coming up with good ideas — of identifying some significant central fact about a product, and then dramatising it in a striking, memorable way.

Several well known companies market packets of seeds for growing vegetables and flowers. Let's suppose that one of them asks you to come up with a creative concept that will give their products a boost.

Talking to them about the product you discover one significant fact. Seeds are *hygroscopic* — which of course means simply that they absorb moisture rapidly. However, dampness reduces the potency of seeds, which means that packaging needs to be impervious to moisture if the seeds are to remain bone dry until the moment the packet is opened.

As so often, research into the product suggests a creative approach — in this case a concept that dramatises the integrity of the packets in which the seeds are sold.

The concept is summed up in a headline:

**BUGGINS SEEDS ARRIVE RARIN' TO GROW
BECAUSE THEY REACH YOU THIRSTY!**

Beneath this headline, the body copy explains in simple layman's language the critical importance of damp-proof packaging for seeds, and the process by which this firm arrived at its current superior packet. Because this consists of a packet within another packet, it can justifiably be described as "DOUBLE-SEALED". About the evolution of this two-ply pack an interesting story can be told of days when seeds had to be despatched by sea to far-distant parts of the Empire. Then somebody happened to notice that seeds despatched in a lead-lined container arrived in much better condition than the identical product despatched in wooden crates. The reason was of course that while crates admitted damp, the lead-lined casks were impervious to moisture — a discovery that propelled Buggins into the lead.

Quite apart from providing an opportunity to exploit the value of a true and interesting anecdote, this emphasis on a double-sealed package has another advantage. While most people might find it hard to believe that there is any significant horticultural variation in the quality of different brands of seed, they might well find it credible that differences in packaging can affect the product's quality.

This little case history provides a good example of the process by which advertising ideas can be formulated. Close study of the product and the form in which it arrives on the market uncover two key facts: first, that seeds are hygroscopic, and consequently that they need protection from moisture right up until the moment when a gardener opens the packet.

These facts can be dramatised by drawing attention both to the prodigious "thirst" of seeds and the moisture-proof properties of the "double-sealed" packet. (This is one instance where an apparently secondary feature — the product packaging — justifies star billing, and suggests a significant competitive advantage ... which is of course that Buggins' seeds are "thirstier" than other brands because they are better protected from damp.)

There is also, by way of a copywriting bonus, an interesting anecdote to be told about the lead-lined casks, and the part they played in revealing the crucial importance of damp-proof packaging.

The impression given by this whole approach is that Buggins' seeds in their moisture-proof packets arrive in peak condition — awaiting only the first kiss of moisture in order to commence with unimpaired vitality and zest the germination process. Add only the further significant facts that the seeds are 'harvested in peak condition" from "pedigree plants" and packed in a bone-dry environment, and you have the ingredients of a selling message that conveys in vivid, believable terms a picture of product quality.

Even if every other brand of seeds is packaged in just the same way, the fact that Buggins has been the first to explain it in its advertising is likely to give the brand a valuable competitive edge.

Take next the case of a motoring organisation that wishes to consolidate, by advertising in various media, its dominance of a national market in which several organisations are competing for the allegiance of motorists who wish to be assured of prompt assistance should they or their families have the misfortune to break down on the road.

A copywriter might very well begin by recognising how motorists perceive a breakdown: to be suddenly immobilised in the middle of a journey is, for the victim, to be faced with an emergency.

Now help in an emergency is associated in everybody's mind with what are commonly described as "the emergency services" — fire, police and ambulance. None of these can be called on in the event of a simple breakdown on the roads involving neither injury nor fire, nor any criminal offence. But if a breakdown is nevertheless perceived as an emergency, could not an organisation that can be called on for assistance legitimately be termed "an emergency service"? And by describing this organisation as "the 4th emergency service" two goals have been achieved. One is to position it as the national leader — on a par with the essential and much-admired fire, police and ambulance services. The second achievement is to establish this service — and therefore, by extension, the right to call upon it — as *essential*.

This clever idea provided other significant opportunities. One was to make possible the device of printing on the side of the organisation's rescue vehicles, and in advertisements, the familiar pattern of hatching displayed on most police cars and on the bands that policemen wear around their caps. The colours were of course different to those used by the police. Nevertheless, the combination of this 'emergency service" symbol with the claim to be "the 4th emergency service" must have helped enormously to establish the AA's pre-eminence — the obvious choice for motorists in need of help.

The next example of the creative process is a letter that sets out to sell Household Contents insurance.

Here the copywriter's starting point was an attempt to present the somewhat abstract concept of insurance in terms of the unpleasant reality of a three-fold risk that every household faces — fire, flood and burglary. At the same time, he had to bear in mind the need to convince his readers of the dangers of being under-insured.

If your home was burgled, would it be <u>your</u> money that the thieves made off with?

. . . Or if you had a fire, would it be <u>your</u> money that went up in smoke?

. . . Or if you were flooded, would it be <u>your</u> money that gurgled down the drain?

"Not likely!" you might think; "My home and its contents are insured."

Of course, if you <u>aren't</u> insured the answer, in each case, would be "Yes". The entire cost of replacing what you'd lost would descend on you.

But what if you <u>are</u> insured? "Surely", you might think, "the insurance money would replace the loss in full?"

Well, the disturbing news I must give you is that the answer is probably "No". Almost certainly the insurance money would not cover in full what it would cost you to replace your loss — whether this was clothes, a home, furniture or cash.

In fact, your present insurance cover would be about as useful as half a crash helmet would be to a motor cyclist — or a canopy with a gaping hole in it to a parachutist.

How, you may ask can this be?

The answer is because you are most likely under-insured. Most people are. Insurance companies estimate that no fewer than x per cent of household insurance policies are for sums that fall well below the full current costs of re- placement.

If yours is among them, you are in a dangerous position.

But don't worry. You can protect yourself easily, quickly and quite painlessly. I will tell you how in a moment. But first let me explain just why you could be the loser if your home was broken into, or damaged by fire, flood or storm.

Another example:

If you ever came home to be greeted by the stench of sod- den carpet . . . the acrid smell of fire-blackened furniture or the heartbreak of obscenities scrawled in lipstick on a mir- ror, you would not need to be reminded of the importance of household contents insurance.

One more example, this time an encyclopaedia. Obviously what this contains is an assemblage of knowledge in many dif- ferent fields — science, mathematics, medicine, sport, the arts and many more. The purpose for which readers will use it is to secure information. That, at least, is the justification that they will give themselves if your mailing succeeds in convincing them they ought to buy the book. In reality, the book — or, more likely, set of books — will probably sit gathering dust on many a bookshelf — a silent testimony to the owners' respect for knowledge and their thirst for information.

However, since the whole concept of an encyclopaedia — or for that matter any work of reference — is liable to seem some- what dry and academic, what is needed is a creative approach that helps to make it seem a little more dynamic — something that lends an air of immediacy and urgency to the act of con- sulting an encyclopaedia. Potential readers should be able to see themselves using the product with advantage — helped to perceive its relevance to a range of credible people and situations.

Such considerations combine to trigger the idea of a brochure whose front cover would feature photographs of a range of home and workplace situations, each occupying a panel of its own, and with an appropriate caption drawing attention to one of the many uses of the book. Thus, for example, a child of school age might be pictured consulting the book, beneath the caption "Look Up A Date!" The captions to the other photographs would combine to build up a picture of a work with many uses: "Look Up A Fact!" "Look Up People!" "Look Up Places!" The photographs would depict, not only credible domestic situations such as reading or doing a crossword, but also somebody in an office writing a report.

A brochure with such a cover should succeed in conveying at a glance not only the variety of content, but also the range of situations in which it could be useful, and the different types of people who might profitably use it.

The book itself might also be featured on the cover — shown as the essential key that unlocks the door for all these people to all these benefits.

My last example, too, comes from the insurance field — this time personal injury insurance. Given the task of selling cover for a risk that most people would prefer not to contemplate at all, what kind of creative solution can the copywriter devise?

Obviously, injury or disablement in the home or on the roads is not the kind of eventuality that lends itself to credible or effective illustration. Photographs, even of models feigning injury would be unpleasant and off-putting. Does this fact rule out illustrations altogether?

Not necessarily. What about featuring photographs of people in situations that *could* lead to injury . . . for example cycling, climbing a ladder or crossing a road . . . captioned in quotation marks with the kind of surprised and regretful remarks that other people tend to make about accident victims:

He was so proud of his new bike . . .

He had only gone up to clear the gutter . . .

She had just popped out to the shops . . . .

By such means the key point about the ever-present risk of injury could be made without a hint of spilt blood or splintered bone or unconvincing photographs of models feigning incapacitating injury.

The quest for an idea in some respects resembles what happens when a bucket of water is emptied onto a dusty surface. Rivulets spread out in various directions, with the largest following the paths of least resistance. Other analogies that come to mind are the process of lighting a fuse and then watching it splutter its way towards the ultimate explosion, or lobbing stones into a pond and following the progress of the ripples they create.

The pursuit of an idea often begins by focusing on some aspect of the target area — such as, for example, the risk or reality of damage to household possessions, and then allowing the mind to set off on a path of free association, following at a respectful distance wherever it may lead, taking note along the way of potentially interesting diversions or alternative paths.

It is worth exploring every possibility that comes to mind, including an arresting metaphor or a striking play on words. Later, when all these possibilities are spread before you (fleshed out, where possible, with copy) like cards laid out before the player of a game of patience you can begin the process of editing and rearrangement — assigning this sentence to a letter, that one to a brochure on the grounds that it provides opportunities for illustration.

Effective mailing pieces are often built up, layer upon layer, by a continuous process of development and adaptation. The best brochures and letters are constructed by a painstaking process of fitting together in effective sequences and patterns a large number of individual components consisting of copy and concepts.

Chapter 3

Creative Levers

When you are facing a blank screen or writing pad with a mind that may be just as blank, it may hearten you to remember that there are several creative techniques that you can use to get off to a good start — conceptual levers that you can pull to get the creative juices flowing. Depending on the nature of the product or service that you are selling, it can be useful to consider, one by one, each of the following approaches (they are not, of course, mutually exclusive and you may well find that more than one of them is appropriate).

Promise

A powerful copy lever is a promise. Advertisements and mailing packages, like political manifestos, should embody every pledge that you are confident of being able to deliver:

> *If, within a year, you haven't managed to save many times the cost, we will refund your money in full, without question!*

> *If you can find the same quality anywhere else at a lower price, we'll refund the difference!*

The promise you make need not relate primarily to a refund. Your pledge can take the form of an assurance that some important goal *will* be achieved.

You will be able to speak in public with ease and confidence . . .

You'll enjoy a new sense of fitness and wellbeing . . .

Within six months you will be able to make your wishes known in the language of the country — in restaurants, garages and shops — and will understand what the natives say to you . . .

So easy to follow are these new, large-scale maps that you'll be able to plan your route with confidence, and reach your destination swiftly.

Benefits

What people are looking for in any purchase that they contemplate are *benefits/rewards*. Of these there are of course many kinds, which is why it will pay you to run through in your mind the various categories of benefit that whatever you are trying to sell might be able to provide.

One is obviously *improvement*. The concept of betterment — improvement — can (depending on the nature of the product) be applied in many areas of life, among them health, wealth, education, relationships, parenthood, employment, professional, sporting and artistic skills.

Another kind of benefit falls within a category which might be described, somewhat pompously, as *alleviation*. The situation or condition for which someone may be seeking relief might be medical, physical, social, educational or legal; the point is the extent to which whatever you are selling offers a credible prospect of alleviating pain, discomfort, anxiety or some other type of affliction.

What rewards can you plausibly dangle in front of your prospects? Depending on the nature of your offer, they might include any of these benefits:

- Savings

- Status

- Comfort

- Improved health and fitness

- Enhanced physical attraction

- Fluency (in speech or writing)

- Security (physical or financial)

- Entertainment

- Amusement

- Nostalgia

- Peace of mind

- Capital appreciation

- Knowledge

- Wealth

- Prestige

- Admiration.

The secret of persuading readers to buy can be summed in one simple equation:

$$\frac{\text{Benefits}}{\text{Price}} = \text{Value}$$

What readers do subconsciously is divide *Benefits* by *Price*. The result is the *Value* they place on the product you are selling. So the more benefits you can pack into your letter and brochure, the higher the value of your product in the reader's estimation.

If, in his eyes, the benefits outweigh the price you have probably made a sale. It's as simple as that.

What do I mean by "benefits"? Let's look at an example: A book on gardening. Its distinctive feature is that it contains full-colour photographs of 1,000 garden plants and flowers.

Is that a benefit? The answer is No — it is *not* a benefit: it's a *product feature*. The *benefit* is that the reader can use the photographs to *identify plants*. He can use the book to put names to the plants he sees in parks and gardens. And he can use it to see what plants which are described but not pictured in catalogues would *look like* in his garden.

Benefits are product features looked at from the reader's point of view. Remember that he doesn't give a damn what has gone into the product. The only thing that interests him is what he'll get out of it. Learn to look at every product and service from the buyer's point of view — to try and relate it to needs and situations in the reader's life — make it easy for him to see how he and his family will benefit from having it.

Remember that the reader is going to divide the benefits you will offer by the price you ask him to pay. Remember, too, that there is more to *price* than the money you ask him to pay.

There is, for example, the delay in receiving the product that you want him to buy. If he buys something in a shop, he can take it home that day. With direct mail he has to wait. This disadvantage is part of the price.

There's the gamble of buying something that he hasn't actually seen and handled. In direct mail that's part of the price. There's the consideration that he may be buying from an organisation he may not have dealt with before — or even heard of. That, too, can be seen as part of the price.

Your letter has therefore to do everything possible to minimise in the reader's eyes all these other elements of "price". *Guarantees . . . testimonials . . . approval . . . money-back promises . . . cancellation privileges . . . reassurance about the credentials of the vendor* — the company's *reputation* and *trustworthiness*: all these are devices for making price seem smaller, for making benefits loom larger, for making *value* seem higher — in fact for giving copy the dimension of *credibility*.

Empowerment

One of the keys to selling is what might be termed "empowerment" — convincing the reader that buying something will be an "enabling act" in the sense that its possession will enable him to do something that he badly wants to do, but hasn't so far been able to achieve, whether this is playing better golf, growing bigger tomatoes or helping children to do better at school. Everybody has aspirations and ambitions. Successful copywriters set out to identify these aspirations, and build bridges for the reader — bridges constructed from features of the product that will carry people from where they are now to where they would like to be.

There are some services and products to which it might seem difficult to relate the concept of "empowerment". But with a little thought it is nearly always possible. Take for example a laundry service — how could using it "empower" customers?

The answer is by enabling them to make important savings. With the time and energy that they save by farming out to someone else such tedious chores as ironing and washing they will be able to do more enjoyable, important and interesting things.

That at least is the enticing prospect that you can hold out to them — and it is the justification that they will be able to use in order to stifle any residual feelings of guilt that some people might have about paying others to do what they could so easily do for themselves. Of course, in reality, they may well spend all the time saved watching television, rather than going on country walks, taking a part-time job, reading improving books or listening to Brahms.

This discrepancy between aspiration and reality illustrates an important fact about human motivation, and one that is directly related to this concept of empowerment. It is that the aspiration is often some goal that will never be achieved, even if the aspirant were suddenly to acquire the means to achieve it.

The stuff of many an impulse to purchase is dreams — the purchaser's private dream of personal or family betterment or accomplishment. Many a tool kit and do-it-yourself book is gathering dust, unused, on the owner's shelves bought on impulse in pursuit of some dream of self-reliant skills. Countless captive bicycles, skiing and rowing machines bear reproachful witness to abandoned resolutions to embark on fitness programmes, while costly sets of golf clubs languish in cupboards all over the world, bought in pursuit of dreams of sporting prowess.

The point is that all these purchases were originally made because the buyers saw each purchase as an enabling act — a bridge between where they already were and where they dreamed of being. So it matters little whether the bridge that you build leads to some hard-nosed actual achievement, or just the dream of one, so long as the product you are selling is presented as a plausible means of conveyance.

Change

Change can be a powerful copywriting gambit. Very often it pays to remind the reader how much time, and things, have changed — to remind people that new knowledge, new techniques, new materials, new tools, new treatments, new plants, and new products are now available that are superior to their predecessors. This emphasis on change and obsolescence provides an opportunity to explain why your product is "state of the art".

Here are one or two examples of the use of this approach.

> I am sure that £40,000 seemed a more than adequate sum when you took out your policy with us in 1985. Since then of course inflation has combined with rising prices to reduce substantially the current purchasing power of the sum assured.

In the case of a life insurance policy, the letter might continue:

> So we thought that, as your 50th birthday approaches, you might welcome an opportunity to bring your policy in

line with the current cost of living by "topping up" the sum assured. And provided that you do this before your birthday you will still enjoy the benefit of the significantly lower premium payable at age 49.

If the policy covers household contents, the second paragraph might read:

And since in the intervening years you have probably acquired several new and valuable possessions, we thought that you might welcome this reminder that it is always wise to keep your household contents insurance up to date. By taking care to have your possessions adequately covered, you avoid any risk of the substantial penalties of being under-insured.

Emphasis on change can also help to sell a car:

It is now several years since you made what I hope you still consider an excellent investment: your Bobcat 3.5 convertible.

Fine car that it is, the Bobcat has held its value well — one reason, I thought, why you might think that this is the right moment to consider replacing your vehicle with the current model. Not only are we able to quote you a good price for the car that you would be replacing; you would also be buying a model that is, in many respects, significantly better . . . safer, faster, more economical — and even better-looking.

Here's how the concept of change can be used in an approach to gardeners:

This letter brings you a warm invitation to a special Open Day that we plan to hold shortly at the Pink Hydrangea Garden Centre. If you have not been to see us lately (our records show that you made your last purchase in 1995)

**you will, I think be both surprised and delighted at the
changes you will find.**

**In recent years the whole garden scene has changed dra-
matically; new tools and materials have come on the market that make gardening less of an effort and even more of
a pleasure. And the many stunning new varieties of plants
that are now available include several that are notable for
their robust resistance to pests and diseases, as well as for
their capacity to withstand extremes of climate.**

**To encourage you to pay us a visit, and by way of saying
"Welcome!" to our Open Day, I have pleasure in enclosing
a Discount Voucher that you will be able to use to reduce
still further the already highly competitive prices of the
huge range that we shall have on display.**

Challenge

If it seems appropriate to the nature of your offer, one creative
technique worth considering is to confront your reader with a
challenge. This challenge should be one to which he is probably not equal — but of a kind that the product you are selling
will enable him to meet.

Suppose, for example, that you have some sort of health
product to promote — an exercise machine, perhaps, or a
"health and fitness" publication. "Can you put your socks on
without sitting down?" might be an appropriate challenge to
the overweight . . . or "Can *you* get up from a chair without using its arms or your own?"

Or maybe you are selling financial advice: "Can you spot the
six early warning signs of impending financial disaster?"
sounds like the kind of challenge that those who don't want to
risk losing their shirts will want to be equipped to meet.

The gap that yawns between people's ambitions and their
actual achievements is a fruitful area for exploration. "Are the
tomatoes that you grow always big and firm?" is a question to
challenge the skills of any gardener. And it doesn't take great

imagination to think of other areas in which people might be sensitive about size and firmness, and vulnerable to a challenge that is not posed too brutally — so long as the product that you are selling offers a credible prospect of remedying perceived deficiencies.

Most of us are uneasily aware of potentially embarrassing gaps in our fund of competence and knowledge, and an intelligent copywriter will make the reader believe that his feelings of inadequacy are both natural and understood. Suppose, again, that you are promoting a book about first aid. Obviously you would write about all the prompt and helpful first aid measures that the book could equip readers to take. But the fastest and easiest way to convince potential buyers of its value might well be to confront the reader with an all-too-common situation in which, right now, he would probably be unable to cope.

> Here's a guide that will spare you that shame-faced, helpless feeling of inadequacy when you find yourself caught up in a situation where someone needs help urgently but your lack of first aid knowledge makes you unable to provide it . . . for example if the person ahead of you in the street suddenly collapses, or you are the first to arrive on the scene of a traffic accident, and find one of the victims bleeding copiously from her injuries.

Which of us hasn't at some time or other felt inadequate? And which of us couldn't be persuaded to invest in something that could spare us having to live through such a humiliating experience again?

Here is some copy that brings home to the reader the frustrating, embarrassing reality of not being able to speak a foreign language.

> The ability to communicate easily with others — to make our wishes and feelings known to them, and to understand what they say to us — is something that most of us take for granted when we are in Britain. But as soon as we

venture across the Channel, life can become much more difficult for those without some knowledge of a foreign language.

In business meetings . . . if a police car, siren screaming, waves you to a halt . . . if your car breaks down and you have to take it to a garage . . . in restaurants and bars . . . those who cannot speak or understand the language of the country quickly develop a new understanding of that sense of isolation felt by those who have some speech or hearing handicap. If you can't communicate with others you are effectively both deaf and dumb — and suffering a handicap no less frustrating for being self-imposed.

Imagine, then, the marvellous sense of liberation that will be your reward for sending for our language course. Just a few minutes every day spent listening to these tapes will rapidly loosen your tongue, enabling you to hold conversations with fluency and ease.

It hardly seems necessary to add that it is never smart to throw down challenges that people may feel unable to meet, unless you swiftly go on to offer something that provides the means to do so.

Novelty

A powerful word in the salesman's vocabulary is "New!" If you can plausibly present what you are offering as new, or at least as incorporating significant new features, it will pay you to emphasise the element of novelty: "Never before an insurance policy that provides so much protection!" "The first screwdriver to incorporate a torch!" In a competitive, technological world consumers have been conditioned to expect constant innovation — they rapidly tire of products they regard as everyday, commonplace — "old hat". Hence of course the appearance on supermarket shelves of so many familiar old brands in new packets emblazoned with new names — or at least old names with the magic prefix "NEW!"

Much successful copy creates an impression of a product that breaks old moulds or new ground — pushes frontiers back.

Change the vowel in new to replace e with o, and you have another powerful advertising word. "<u>Now</u> with added vitamins" . . . "<u>Now</u> available in your choice of six attractive colours" . . . implying as it does immediacy, contemporaneity, superiority to what has gone before, *now* is a good word to use when new would not be justified.

Exclusivity

Even if it isn't new, can you at least justify a claim that your product is *exclusive* — obtainable only from you? Or if it is widely available does it incorporate exclusive features? Is there anything about your product that enables you to claim that it is unique? If what you sell is in no way exclusive, maybe the terms on which you are able to offer it are — the price may be lower, or perhaps your offer includes a free gift or the chance to win a prize. It is worth digging hard to see if you can justify a claim that your offer — if not the actual product — is *exclusive*.

Topicality

Another useful creative lever, which you can use in conjunction with many of those described above, is *topicality* — making contact with people at a time when they are most likely to be receptive to your message, and therefore interested in what you have to offer. This is easier with some products or services than others, but for those which provide a credible opportunity to use it, this approach can strengthen the impact of your offer. Some events and actions are predictable: for example, spring bulbs come into flower (obviously enough) in spring. Tax bills, assessments and returns go out at the same time every year. People are likely to be most fearful of the consequences of their car breaking down at the time of year when they are about to set off on holiday.

Here are one or two examples of headlines which make use of this element of topicality:

WANT TO PAY LESS TAX NEXT YEAR?
New Guide Explains 10 Legal Ways To Slash Your Tax Bill

DISAPPOINTED WITH YOUR SHOW OF
SPRING BULBS THIS YEAR?
Take The First Crucial Steps Today To Ensure
A Stunning Display Next Year

Note how in each case a topical challenge is followed by the promise of a benefit.

Comparison

Not many of the things that you are called upon to sell will be unique. This means that you will need to compare them carefully with their competitors in the hope of discovering features that make them arguably superior. Even if it is in all significant respects identical to most similar products or services on offer, you might still be able to identify some feature which — appropriately dramatised — makes it *seem* superior.

An old but true story tells of a copywriter who was given the job of selling beds. Naturally, the advertising pitch he chose was the comfort of beds manufactured by the client. On the obligatory factory visit, he learned that both the base and mattress incorporated several layers of springs — a feature which although common, too, to all the competitors' beds, had never previously been mentioned in their advertising.

This discovery gave the writer the inspiration that he sought: "Springs sprung on springs!" rang the slogan he created for his client, which became (if I may so describe it) the mainspring of a highly successful campaign.

Opposites

Depending on the nature of what you are trying to sell, using extremities or opposites can be a useful device. The extremes can be alphabetical, geographical, or of any other kind that seems appropriate to the nature of the product. The intention is the same: to convince your prospects that what you are offering is complete and comprehensive — that it covers the waterfront in a satisfying way.

Thus in the case of an atlas you might promise:

> **From Aden to Zanzibar, from the North Pole to the South ... find your way easily round the world with this new and up-to-date reference work.**

Or of a cookery course:

> **From Thai dishes to nouvelle cuisine, from hearty farmhouse cooking to cuisine minceur, from an impromptu supper to a formal dinner party . . . here are appetizing, healthy dishes to delight your family and friends.**

The examples that you use can be false or arbitrary in the sense that they are not really opposites. The device is really no more than another way of saying "Here is everything you need" — a slightly less space-consuming alternative to giving a list of examples, followed by the dreary "etc, etc," or "and much, much more!"

Anecdotes

People love to read a story. One proven device for grabbing the attention of your readers, and — no less crucial — for *holding* their interest, is to tell a story. Naturally the story needs to have a point, and to have direct relevance to whatever you are selling.

> **A few weeks ago I was driving along a deserted country road in Norfolk. The day was bitterly cold, and I felt in need of a hot drink. So, pulling in to the side of the road, I poured myself a cup of coffee from the Thermos flask. A few minutes later, refreshed and warmed, I adjusted the seat belt and turned the key in the ignition. Not a sign of life! Again and again I turned the key, but to my consternation the car refused to start. No lights appeared on the instrument panel, no sound could be heard from the en-**

> gine. With mounting anxiety and irritation I faced up to
> the fact that I was marooned miles from anywhere in a
> desolate landscape.
>
> How glad I was then to remember the mobile telephone
> stashed away in the glove compartment. Within seconds I
> was in touch with the (motoring organisation) listening to
> the calm voice of the operator assuring me that help
> would be on hand in minutes.

A story and situation like this is one with which readers can
easily identify. It will remind any motorist of the risk and the
reality of a breakdown on the road — possibly in a remote, inconvenient or even dangerous place. If he is not yet a member
of a motoring organisation he will be receptive to the case you
go on to make for joining one.

And here is another anecdote — used now to explain to the
maybe sceptical reader the reason why he is being offered
chances to win in a sweepstake.

> A young trainee teacher was being shown round a school
> by the Headmaster. Entering one noisy classroom the
> Head picked up a long ruler and slammed it on the nearest
> pupil's desk.
>
> In the ensuing silence the astonished young teacher whis-
> pered to her elder "At college we were taught to keep dis-
> cipline by talking to them!"
>
> "Of course, my dear" replied the Head, "But first you have
> to get their attention!"
>
> That's why we offer you these chances to win in our
> sweepstakes — to bring your attention to an offer that we
> think you'll find of interest.

Evocation

For some products — among them books, foods, videos, holidays and music — the process of evocation can be a useful tool. The evocation of things that appeal to the senses — sight, touch, taste, smell and hearing — can if it is done with skill and sensitivity be surprisingly effective. But the conditions — skill and sensitivity — are crucial. A word picture that has been clumsily drawn excites nothing but derision.

> What pictures this music conjures up of Viennese romance and elegance during the benign reign of the Royal Family of the Waltz: beautiful women in gowns of swirling satin, silk and taffeta swept literally off their dainty feet by gorgeously uniformed partners to the exhilarating strains of a waltz by Johann Strauss . . . the soft glow of a dozen sparkling chandeliers reflected in gilded mirrors on the silk-hung walls . . . heady scents of costly perfumes, mingling with the aroma of a choice cigar.

> Norway's landscape would tax the vocabulary of a poet. Wherever you look, you'll see some sight to make you catch your breath: towering glaciers gleaming a blue-green colour in the sunlight; snow-capped mountains mirrored in the waters of a fjord; trim farmsteads clinging to mountain slopes. Hardly anywhere in the country are you out of sight of water: majestic rivers, tumbling streams, cascading waterfalls . . . and everywhere sunlight glinting on the waters of a lake.

> To nerves and muscles tautened by the pace and strain of life, we offer a landscape which might have been designed to soothe the senses. The silence of the forests and the grandeur of the mountains — above all, perhaps, the natural, unspoiled beauty of the fjords — combine to create an atmosphere of deep, abiding peace.

UPSTAIRS MEALS AT DOWNSTAIRS PRICES!
"What better beginning to a meal — family lunch or formal
dinner party — than a plate of succulent smoked salmon?

Just the sight of those tender slices — pink and succulent —
puts everyone in a good mood . . . helps to create a real
sense of occasion, and promotes a sensation of well being.

A squeeze of lemon to taste . . . a sprinkling of freshly
milled black pepper . . . surely this must have been the
food the gods called 'ambrosia'.

All very well, you may be thinking, but what of the expense? Isn't smoked salmon prohibitively costly — an occa-
sional treat when you go out for a celebration meal, not a
delicacy within the reach of your regular housekeeping
budget?

If that's what you're thinking, AB of   have good news
for you. By marrying the most up-to-the-minute scientific
know-how with traditional skills and techniques, this
company has succeeded in farming the lordly salmon.

First, the salmon are cured in the age-old way with salt,
dark Caribbean rum and rich demerara sugar. Then they
are smoked in the time-honoured fashion that has made
smoked salmon from Scotland so highly esteemed
throughout the world . . . over gently-smouldering chips of
hand-picked oak and juniper. The result: an incomparable
delicacy, unique in flavour as it is in quality. A heavenly
dish at a down-to-earth price that brings it within your
reach.

Word pictures help to trigger nostalgia — an emotion that can
often help to clinch a sale.

In this connection it is worth bearing in mind that people don't
only feel nostalgic for things that they themselves remember. It
is possible, too, to experience a feeling of nostalgia for what is
essentially a collective or folk memory — an experience so often

recounted and described that even those who never had it *feel*
that they have done so, and can in consequence feel nostalgia for
it. The war years yield many examples, as also for many people
do the Twenties, Thirties and — more recently — the Sixties.

Lift Words

In the examples above you will have noticed certain words that
lift and lend colour to the passage as a whole. The choice and
positioning of such words is a significant aspect of the copywriter's craft. Like the herbs and spices used by cooks they add
flavour to the copy; and, to pursue the analogy further, they
need to be used with a little restraint — otherwise they become
too obtrusive and tend to mask the flavour.

Flattery

A difficult one to bring off without sounding false or smarmy;
but if you can manage it a highly effective approach.

> *Many more than is commonly supposed are gifted with an
> appreciation of fine art. Less common are those with the
> means to indulge their taste.*

> *If you have been lucky enough to cultivate an eye and taste
> for water colours, you will not need to be reminded that
> one of the foremost contemporary exponents of the art —
> an artist of international renown — is the Libyan painter . . . .*

> *And if you are fortunate enough to be blessed as well with
> the means to gratify your taste, you will, I think, welcome
> the opportunity this letter brings you: an opportunity to
> acquire at an affordable price one or two of a strictly lim-
> ited edition of superb silk-screen prints of his work. There
> are of course many whose taste in art runs to nothing
> more distinguished or individual than mass-produced re-
> productions of the work of celebrated painters.*

> *Others — you, I believe among them — delight in acquiring
> works by contemporary painters of distinction before their*

work is priced out of reach. Such acquisitions are, at the least, an investment in pure pleasure which offers, too, the possibility of financial gain. And if the original does not always lie within our reach, it is today possible to acquire the painting in a form so true and faithful to it that even the eye of an expert is sometimes hard put to tell the difference.

Or again:

You will soon be seeing — in the Press and on TV — news of a highly significant addition to the bank's range of services to customers.

And before you read elsewhere about the gold card, I want you — as one of the bank's most respected and substantial customers — to have the news direct from me, together with a formal invitation to apply for your own personal card.

Do not, I urge you, be misled by the title of this new card. This bank's gold card is not just another piece of gilded plastic for the status conscious, who like to impress shop assistants and head waiters with some visible token of their wealth.

Our card takes over where the other gold cards stop, and confers on the hand-picked holder benefits more solid and substantial than prestige.

Quite simply, it gives the holder immediate access to a superior range of banking services that no other gold card offers. Because the opportunity to hold the card is being offered only to selected, financially-substantial customers, it is possible to offer a uniquely attractive range of benefits.

Frights and Rights

One subject of endless and inconclusive debate is the question of which provides the stronger motivation — *hope of gain* or

fear of loss. Both provide powerful levers for impelling people
to take action. And I would suggest that both, where appropriate, ought to be considered. In the case of sweepstakes offers
both can be brought into play. If the reader is sent numbers in a
draw that has already taken place, failure to send them back for
checking could result in him forfeiting a prize that he would
have been able to claim. Fear of losing to someone else money
that could have been his obviously provides a powerful motive
to reply. If the draw is to be held at some time in the future,
hope of gain alone should persuade him to respond. And it is
perfectly feasible to feature both a pre- and a post- draw in a
single mailing package.

The question crops up again in the context of many other
kinds of product and service, among them several in the health
field such as insurance, exercise machines, health books and
the like. Is it more effective to dwell on the spectre of ill health
that such products can help users to avoid, or on the more
cheerful prospect of radiant good health that they can promote?

Or again take the example of a magazine for consumers.
There are many positive features:

> **Get better value in the shops . . .**

> **Choose better and safer investments . . .**

> **Find out if you are paying too much tax — are there valu-
> able allowances that you can claim?**

But frights too come into the picture:

> **Dodgy investments that could prove catastrophic . . .**

> **Electrical appliances that are unsafe . . .**

Where to place the main emphasis depends of course on the
nature of the product, and on the relative strengths of the ideas
that you come up with to promote it. My instinct would be to go
for both frights and rights (the alternatives are not mutually ex-

clusive, even though marketing people often talk as if they were, prattling portentously about "hard" and "soft" approaches). Successful promotion is nearly always based on a cocktail of approaches. But if I were forced to make a choice, my preference would be for frights as the stronger motivation.

Finding a Framework

One problem that all copywriters face is that of providing some suitable framework for all the points that they want to make about whatever they are selling. Without some such structure your copy can soon easily become an incoherent mass of verbiage. The device of using categories provides a natural framework round which to organise copy.

Every individual fills a number of different roles: for example, parent, employee, voter, patient, consumer, partner, passenger — and so on. If your product — say a newsletter or a book — is relevant to, and of value in, several of these roles a useful device is to take them, one by one, and explain the relevant benefits that it offers each of them.

Alternatively, instead of being of value to one individual in several different roles, a product may be of value to several different categories of user, for example, lawyers, accountants, financial advisers, teachers. Again, a useful device for structuring your sales pitch is to take each category in turn and explain the value and relevance of the product that you are selling to each.

One more device for structuring a sales pitch is to look at a variety of realistic situations — at work, in the home, on the road, at school — and wherever else a product may be relevant, and explain its potential value in each.

This device of using categories is especially useful when you have the opportunity to illustrate — as in the case of a leaflet or brochure.

Chapter 4

Creative Tools (1):
Writing Effective Letters

A letter supplies the element of *personal contact*. Unlike brochures and press ads, which are obviously public forms of communication, a letter can be made to seem personal and private — particularly if it can be personalised, not just with the recipient's name and address but also by using information from the database, such as previous purchases made from you, or the tastes and interests that can reasonably be deduced from them. (If somebody has bought garden plants he is probably interested in gardening — and, by extension, in nature and the outdoors).

Because they are personal, the best letters have an easy, direct, conversational tone. "Write as you speak!" is a piece of sound advice to bear in mind when you are writing a letter. Another useful tip is to follow the practice of successful public speakers who know how to give a talk (that has in fact been meticulously scripted) an appearance of easy spontaneity by building into it various passages that are calculated to seem informal and impromptu. And just as these speeches are written to be spoken, it can be useful for a writer to see how a letter written to be read sounds when spoken aloud. If it sounds easy and conversational in tone, these qualities will probably come across when it is read. Conversely, if it sounds stilted, pompous or contrived that is how it will seem to the reader.

A letter, then, can be likened to one half of a dialogue, whereas a brochure is more like a public performance. While I wouldn't want to push the analogy too far, there is a sense in which the reader of a letter does participate in a form of dialogue with the writer. This is because by the very act of responding to your offer the reader is making a statement about the kind of person he is, the problems that concern him, his ambitions and desires, his tastes and interests. And the nature of this statement is heavily influenced by the kind of letter that you write.

It is easy to write of a product or service in a way that can make an order for it seem like a confession of weakness or inadequacy. Health and self-help products are obvious examples of offers that are sometimes made in terms that could make those who accept feel faintly embarrassed or inadequate.

So one quality to be prized in copywriters is a sensitive awareness that the terms in which a product is promoted should enable those who buy it to feel that they are saying something nice about themselves.

I have mentioned the trap of promoting certain kinds of product in a way that can make people feel shy about accepting your offer. Alternatively and more successfully you can take care to persuade them to perceive acceptance as a dynamic statement of a positive approach to life — a declaration of a sensible concern for health, or a wholly commendable desire for self-improvement . . . a confession of ambition rather than inadequacy.

It is difficult to write a decent letter without having in mind a picture of the kind of individual who will (you hope) be reading it. This is where demographics and research have a part to play. What they can tell you about the people who make up your market can help you to build up a kind of composite picture of "the reader".

In the absence of any such guidance about the kind of people to whom you are writing, it is not a bad rule to proceed on the assumption that they are likely to be not all that different to you.

Listen with an inward ear to the hopes that you are addressing and the benefits you promise, and ask yourself how they sound to you. Anything that sounds to you false, discordant, patronising or unbelievable would almost certainly strike a wrong note with most other people too. If you don't have in mind a clear mental picture of another kind of reader, the best thing to do is write a letter to yourself.

Sometimes one comes across a mailing package in which the letter simply paraphrases the brochure. Each says the same things, in much the same sequence, and often in much the same words. This always strikes me as a waste of time and paper. For although both are describing the same proposition, each has a different role to play.

Contrary to a widely held opinion that the crucial element in the package is a colourful brochure, there is evidence that the central component is the *letter*. It supplies the essential element of direct personal contact. The letter is indispensable; while there are many examples of successful mailings that consisted only of a letter, it is hard to think of any that comprised no more than a brochure. Remove the letter from the mailing package and what you have left is what recipients are likely to perceive as a piece of low-grade advertising — a mass-produced hand-out stuffed indiscriminately through their letterboxes.

A well-written letter sponsors and chaperones the other contents of the envelope; in radio terms it is the programme's "presenter". And just as the best broadcasters succeed by sounding as if they are speaking to a friend, skilful copywriters succeed in creating the impression that the letter has been written specifically for the individual to whom it is addressed. It can only do this if the writer can manage to do several things — of which the first and most important is to convince the reader of its relevance to his needs and interests. If the writer can demonstrate in the first few sentences the letter's *relevance*, he will secure the reader's attention and interest. Whether or not the letter features a computer-printed salutation ("Dear Mr

Smith") it will *seem* personal if the initial sentences demonstrate the relevance to the reader of what is on offer.

A good letter ought to *flow*, with paragraphs following each other in logical progression, and the last sentence of one and the first sentence of another skilfully fashioned to fit together like a dovetailed joint. It is also important to give the best news first, and also to provide the essential instructions on how to place an order.

And try to finish with a "clincher". Often one finds a sales letter that closes with an anti-climax or ends on a dying fall. This is probably because by the time he reaches the final paragraph the writer has exhausted his reserves of energy and ingenuity; the creative well-spring has run dry. In that case, put the letter aside and come back fresh to it later to pen some final clincher. "That short walk to the post-box with your order could be one of the most important journeys of your life."

Structuring Letters

Every letter needs a well thought-out structure, a sensible sequential arrangement of the contents. But not every letter has to follow precisely the sequence suggested below, which simply illustrates the components common to most good sales letters.

Headline

First of all, the *Headline*. Ideally, this makes a promise and features highlights of your offer:

> EAT BETTER, CHEAPER EVERY DAY with the *Good Health Cookbook* — Test A Copy On Approval . . . Taste And Feel The Difference!

Salutation

Next, the *Salutation*. This means more than just addressing the reader by name — or calling him "Dear Reader". If you can, it pays to incorporate an element of *recognition*. Where possible, address the reader as a friend and customer. Mention previous products bought from you — particularly *affinity* products. If some previous purchase has defined an area of interest, referring to that interest is an obvious springboard for the offer of another product in that field:

> I know that you bought our *Cook's Companion*. And because we know of your interest in good food you are one of the first to be offered, on approval, our new *Good Health Cookbook*.

Opening

Next, the *Opening*. The first couple of paragraphs are *crucial*. If they fail to engage the reader's interest, your letter will be still-born. This is where you grasp the reader's *attention* and secure a firm grip on his *interest*. It is worth spending a lot of time and thought on the headline and opening paragraphs. Sometimes it takes a few paragraphs to warm up and get into your stride. In such cases you might be well advised when the letter is finished to go back to the beginning and discard the original opening. Often a few later sentences, written when you have warmed to your task, can be seen to make a stronger opening.

Identification

The next stage in the sequence is *Identification*, by which I mean telling the reader what benefits your letter offers:

> Packed with recipes for dishes (300 of them!) that taste just as good as they look, the *Good Health Cookbook* delivers a valuable bonus in the (flatteringly slim-line) shape of better health and greater energy — a new sense of well-being.

Explanation

Next comes further *Explanation* of what the product will do for the reader. *Who will benefit from using it, and how and when it will be used*, especially the needs that it will meet and the situations in which its use will be beneficial and/or enjoyable:

> Packed with ideas for appetising meals that are quick, nourishing and easy to prepare the *Good Health Cookbook* will appeal to every hard-pressed working parent who comes home, tired, to face a hungry family. With recipes chosen from these pages you'll have the huge satisfaction of knowing that the meals you eat are as healthy as the appetites they satisfy. What is more the cooking instructions are so clear and easy to follow that you could easily come home to find a meal already cooked and on the table — prepared by children or a partner for whom the book has kindled a new interest in cooking!

> There are dishes here for all occasions, from a TV supper to a formal dinner party, from a snack lunch for unexpected guests to a special picnic.

Terms of Offer

Now come full details of the terms on which the product is offered. For example:

> The only way to judge a cookery book is to put it to the test in your kitchen. That's why we are now giving you the opportunity to carry out just such a test of the *Good Health Cookbook*. And with ten whole days in which to try it out on approval, without obligation to buy, you and others in the household should have ample time to sample several of these healthy, appetising, satisfying recipes for every kind of dish, from soups to soufflés, as well as for fish, meat, poultry and vegetarian dishes.

People don't like to commit themselves. The value of approval is that it *postpones commitment*. The offer can safely be accepted as "no obligation is involved". If you are making an approval offer, remind the reader constantly of this reassuring fact, that the big decision (whether or not to buy) still lies in the future.

Bargain

Everybody loves a *Bargain*; make the most of any opportunity to convince the reader that he is getting £30 worth for only £25. Show (if you can) how much more your product offers for the money than the competition. If it can fill more than one role, be sure to say so. Exploit the implications of direct sale — no middleman's profit — to explain a discount, or to emphasise value. Remind the reader what else he could buy with the money he is saving. Do everything you can to make the price seem small and the process of paying painless (for example, with an option to pay by instalments).

> **If you decide that the book would prove a valuable addition to your bookshelf, it is yours for a first payment of only £2, followed by 4 monthly payments of £4 each (total, £18). For less than the price of a meal for one in a decent restaurant, you get recipes for 300 tasty, nutritious and above all healthy dishes that everyone in the family will enjoy.**

Sandwich the price between *benefits* and flattering *comparisons*, and what might otherwise seem to the reader quite a lot of money will come to look like a bargain.

Reassurance

This is an important component of your letter, provided by mentioning such features as approval, quality and refund guarantees and the reputation of the vendor. The aim is to deprive timid readers of any excuse *not* to order.

Directions

The final element in the sequence is *directions*: don't forget to give the reader clear instructions on how to place an order. Letters should always close with a *request*. If you fail to provide this, you shouldn't be surprised if people don't respond in the way that you want. Close by telling the reader what you want him to do — what it is in his interests to do:

> **Post the enclosed order form today in the reply-paid envelope provided. And to make sure of your gift of an attractive pepper-mill, post your order <u>today</u>.**

Readability Devices

The first duty of a writer is of course to get the copy *read*. So let's look now at devices for improving *readability* — making life easy for the reader . . . tempting him to read and to *go on reading*. Here are some of them:

- Headlines
- Underlining
- Brackets
- Scoring
- Second colour
- Indenting
- Subheads
- Simulated handwriting
- Asterisks
- Bullets
- Paper stock
- Postscript
- Capitals.

First there is, of course, the *headline* which it is often helpful to print in a second colour.

Another useful device is the headline that summarises benefits. This has the advantage, for people whose lips move when they read, of saving them the trouble of reading the whole letter! They probably wouldn't have read it all anyway, so at least you have made sure that they understand the main points of the offer. Another device is to put key words in *capitals*.

Others include *underlining*, *brackets*, and *scoring* in the margin to emphasise key sentences. Printing in a *second colour*. *Indenting* important sentences or paragraphs. *Simulated handwriting* in the margin — again to emphasise key features. *Asterisks* and *bullets*. Choosing a *paper stock* — for example, antique or dignified — that is in keeping with your message. Plenty of *subheads* not only make a letter look easier to read. Skilfully chosen, they ensure that superficial readers who do no more than skim your letter can nevertheless absorb the salient features at a glance. And lastly another well-tried device is to feature, as a *postscript*, some major benefit or aspect of the offer.

Copy Devices

Most of the features mentioned above are *visual*. There are also some verbal tricks of the trade — *proven* devices for making copy easier to read. These include:

- The **Subhead** featured on the same line as the sentence, rather than above it.

- **Shorts.** Short sentences. Short paragraphs. Incomplete sentences (which of course means a sentence without the three components of a subject, object and a verb). For example: "Not a bit of it!"

- **Heads.** Make liberal use of subheads and cross-heads, choosing them to bring out major features of your product and offer so that the reader can (at a pinch) get the gist of it by scanning the subheads.

- **Quotes.** Wherever possible, use quoted speech. Readers find such passages inviting. They are easy to read.

- **Questions.** Ask direct questions of the reader as a change of pace.

- **Screamers**. Exclamation marks — preferably used with some restraint — add an element of drama.

- **Cases**. Make liberal use of any relevant case histories and human-interest anecdotes.

- **Brackets**. Putting passages in brackets makes for variety, change of pace.

- **Sentence Breaks**. Try to make sure that the end of the page does not coincide with the end of the sentence; readers are more likely to follow the copy overleaf if the last sentence, word or paragraph on the page is broken, obliging them to turn to the next page to continue reading. A page that ends with a full stop provides an escape hatch for the reader!

Tricks of the Trade

Resolving Conflicting Priorities

Often there is more than one important point that you wish to make up-front in a letter. When two or more key features of the offer compete for pole position, the trap to avoid is getting so bogged down in explaining the details of one early in the letter that the other is relegated to a secondary role, with the result that neither makes much impact on the reader.

An effective solution can be to mention them both at the outset, while deferring a full explanation of one to a later paragraph:

> More in a moment about this important feature. But first I would like to tell you about . . .

> But before I tell you more about this attractive gift, I would like for a moment to look at another major benefit.

Cross Selling

Opportunities often arise for introducing customers to services or products that are offered by other divisions or departments of the same organisation, or by another company in the same group. In such cases, a brief letter of introduction from a senior figure in that part of the organisation with whom the customer has already done business can pave the way for valuable additional business with some other department of the business.

> Some time ago we had the pleasure of arranging life insurance for you. It occurs to me that you may well have other insurance needs with which this company would be well placed, and pleased, to help. As a policyholder you may well find it advantageous to ask us to provide a quotation for any of the other forms of insurance we provide. As one of our policyholders you would find that we can quote you highly competitive terms on your Buildings, Household Contents or Motor insurance, as well as on many other forms of more specialised protection such as Sickness or Disability insurance.
>
> As you probably know, European Widgets are part of Global Gizmos — a group of companies that includes — in the shape of National Gizmos — one of this country's leading suppliers of these essential components.
>
> My purpose in writing is therefore to introduce you to the range of high quality products that National Gizmos can offer, and also to give you the good news that, as the customer of a sister company, you could look forward to receiving a substantial discount on any order that you choose to place.

Such letters of introduction from a familiar name are likely to produce a much better response than a cold mailing from the department or company seeking new business.

Hitting the Right Targets

A common explanation for a disappointing result from a mailing is simply a failure to reach the individual who is most likely to be interested in the offer, and who would play the biggest part in any decision to purchase. I have known cookery and medical books to fail because the offers were addressed to a male-dominated list; and conversely offers of do-it-yourself kits to bite the dust because the lists were predominantly female. It is also not uncommon for offers of services and products designed for business use to be totally unsuccessful for no better reason than the fact that they never reached the right person.

So if you think that your offer may be at risk of failing for this reason, you might with a little ingenuity be able to take effective action to ensure that it gets into the right hands (assuming, of course, that you do not know by name who that person is).

One useful stratagem is to head the letter with a box or jog slip containing a message on these lines:

> This offer will be of the greatest interest to whoever in your household/organisation does the cooking/buys the stationery. If that does not happen to be you, may I ask you to pass on this letter to the appropriate colleague/member of your family.

In the field of business-to-business selling, a letter might come with a simulated circulation slip pinned to the top of the first page. This would list the functionaries who might find the offer of interest: Marketing Director, Financial Director, Chief Accountant and so on. Scrawled beneath in simulated manuscript the words "Recommended reading!" followed by some indecipherable initials.

Be Specific

Deal whenever you can in specifics, not generalities. Often one sees advertising claims that would be equally applicable to services or products other than the one for which they are actually being made:

> The ultimate household reference work . . .

> A favourite with gardeners . . .

> The choice of motorists everywhere. . .

It is always more effective to take care that the claims you put forward are seen to relate specifically to what you are selling:

> **Five reasons why [product] is a favourite with organic gardeners . . .**

> **Motorists everywhere choose (product) for the extra mileage and lower service charges it provides.**

Wordplay

Although it is a tool that needs to be used with skill and judgement, a striking or appropriate play on words can be effective in helping you to make a point. "Beanz Meanz Heinz" and "Drinka Pinta Milka Day" are just two examples of memorable advertising slogans that owe their impact to clever manipulation (and deliberate misuse) of the language.

Wordplay does not of course need to involve distorting words as both these examples do. And slogans — however clever — are on the whole of questionable value in a direct mail package or mail order ad. There is, however, room for a play on words that is appropriate to the nature of the product. For example, the front cover of a brochure that was used to promote an unusual kind of dictionary featured just about every possible permutation of the adjectives used in conjunction with "Words" . . . Rude words, Harsh words, Kind words, Words of Wisdom, Words of Congratulation — and so on, to build up a picture of a book that the reader could rely on to supply *le mot juste* for every purpose and occasion.

Another book containing road maps was promoted with a leaflet that showed on the front cover photographs of a range of destinations to which motorists might need help in finding their way. Photographs that showed a seaport, an airfield, a country road and a busy main road were captioned respectively Gangway, Runway, Pretty way, Motorway beneath a head-line inviting the reader to use the book to "FIND YOUR WAY — quickly, easily, economically with this new guide for motorists".

Multiple Function

Where it is possible to do so in a credible fashion it is often useful to portray a product as capable of performing more than one function. For example, you might be justified in claiming of a work of reference that it is "Two books (or at the very least "two *kinds* of book") in one" since it can be used as both a Thesaurus (word-finder) and Dictionary. Of another kind of reference book you might (if it happens to include maps) be justified in claiming that it is both an Encyclopaedia and an Atlas. As well as sucking up dust and crumbs, a vacuum cleaner might be capable of adaptation to the function of blowing fallen autumn leaves into tidy piles, making it easier to sweep them up. It could then be described as "both an essential domestic appliance and a useful garden tool".

If a product has more than one use — is capable of filling several roles — drawing attention to its versatility helps to convince people that it is an excellent buy, offering extra value for their money.

Keep the Product in the Foreground

It is all to easy to fall into the trap of making a stronger case for buying a *category* of product (say, motor insurance) than for buying the specific policy of this specific company.

Avoid this trap by keeping the product you are selling in the foreground — keep mentioning its name. Never mind that many of the benefits it offers are available elsewhere. Just keep connecting them with the product — making sure that you present *this* policy as the key to all the benefits you mention.

You will find in the next chapter copy for a motor-insurer called ROADRISK. Notice how the company's name is mentioned in connection with every benefit.

Make Your Copy Inclusive

Try not to address readers in a way that reveals assumptions on your part that will in many cases prove to be false — for example, an assumption that they are either married or living with a partner or that they have children of their own. However, lots of childless people (godparents, uncles, aunts, etc) are interested in buying things for children as of course are grandparents as well. So it is more tactful to say "Children will enjoy . . ." than "Your children will enjoy . . .". And since many people live in apartments or flats it would be smarter to refer to "Your home" rather than "Your house". Don't make the mistake of assuming that everybody else has the same kind of lifestyle as you, and try to write in a way that will not strike any readers as obviously inappropriate to their circumstances or situation. You are not of course precluded from making claims about the value of a product in a car or in the garden. But since not everyone will have them it would be better not to say *your* garden or *your* car.

Tone of Voice

Much of the difference between First Class Honours and Abject Failure copywriting lies in the tone of voice that you adopt. If more copywriters listened with an inner ear to the patronising drivel that many of them write there would be a great deal less junk in the mails, and the industry's reputation would be a lot higher. Too many writers tend to overlook the fact that braggarts and bores are no more welcome in print than in the flesh. Writing copy is a bit like driving along a narrow road with a deep ditch on either side. It is easy to fall into one of the many traps that lie along your route. Friendliness can seem ingratiating; too serious a tone can come across as pompous or portentous. A light touch can be seen as flippant or facetious.

The tone of your copy should be modulated to suit the nature of your audience. Business-like but relaxed and friendly for a list of average consumers; brisk and no-nonsense for a business list whose members are likely to see themselves as hard-pressed, busy people whose crowded days and diaries leave little time to wade through wordy letters or study elaborate brochures.

This raises another significant issue. People's self-image plays a major role in determining the way they respond to your mailing. The skilful writer takes care to ensure that copy conforms to the likely self-image of readers. So even if they have in fact little to do and ample time to spare for crossword puzzles, a diplomatic writer will be careful to give the impression of not wishing to waste the precious time of busy managers. As we shall see later, the copywriter sometimes needs to be a bit of an actor!

Avoid Obvious Manipulation

People react with understandable hostility to approaches that are too obviously *manipulative*. Blatant appeals to greed, or to a natural concern for the wellbeing of close relatives, can be counter productive. I am not suggesting that a writer should ignore such powerful springs of motivation. What I am saying is that they need to be handled with discretion.

Some mailers who supply envelopes for readers to reply resort to the obvious trick of making the vehicle of acceptance more visually attractive than the one for readers who are not sending an order. People easily see through such obvious attempts at manipulation; they do not like to see the puppet-master's hands or feel the strings being pulled!

Projecting Character

A technique that is sometimes appropriate and useful is to set out deliberately to build up in the reader's mind an agreeable image of the writer. Obviously the mental picture that one attempts to project is of somebody who is both likeable and trustworthy. These should be qualities that distinguish all promotion copy, although it has with reluctance to be recognised that they do not. But I am talking about something more than simply writing copy that is credible and friendly: I mean going one stage further by writing in a way that is sufficiently distinctive and idiosyncratic to convey the flavour of a certain kind of character.

Naturally the personality that one chooses to project needs to be appropriate to the nature of the product — for example, compassionate, caring and concerned in the case of a charity appeal; worldly and cosmopolitan if the mailing is from a travel agency . . . brisk and businesslike if the letter's subject matter concerns the reader's business or profession.

Here is part of a letter from a firm selling wine direct to the consumer, in which the writer is playing the role of a crusty but sympathetic wine merchant of the old school.

> Every year, at just about this time, the prospect of the Budget looms large and menacing. And not only during working hours. Such is the damage done to the wine trade by rapacious Chancellors of both parties, that the approach of Budget Day engenders nightmares. Respectable and sober merchants wake screaming from a dream in which that grinning, beetle-browed face glowers — swollen as a harvest moon — above them, brandishing a red despatch case crammed with new and fiendish taxes.
>
> But as a change from the usual Budget nightmares I had, the other night, a dream of a kind to which psychologists attach the label "wish fulfilment"; I dreamed that the Chancellor told a packed and cheering house:
>
> I propose this year to do something that should have been done long ago. Rejecting totally the advice thrust upon me every year by whey-faced bureaucrats to raise a further piffling sum by increasing the duty on wine, it is my intention to abolish this iniquitous impost altogether. What this country badly needs is a tonic — a restorative, and I can think of none better or more agreeable than wine . . . which from now on shall flow in the land as copiously as North Sea Oil, to enrich, enliven and encourage a people grown weary of politicians' exhortations, and economic gloom — raising their spirits, and liberating their energies and talents.
>
> (At this point, to thunderous applause, the Chancellor pauses for refreshment from a flask containing, not the traditional milksop's potion, but the best part of a bottle of good red Burgundy.)

"It won't ever happen of course. The grimmer but, alas, far more likely prospect is that once again the duty on wine will be increased. So, since this is your last opportunity to order before the Budget, may I urge upon you the wise precaution of sending an order as large as you can possibly afford — including in it perhaps, the five splendid wines in our Budget Selection.

The impersonation in print of real or imaginary people is a significant aspect of the copy-writer's job. It is called for again when a letter purports to come from a celebrity or public figure — as in the case of some appeals for charity. Less plausibly, one often finds a letter signed by a celebrity being used to endorse — or even sell — a product. Whether or not the celebrity's name is associated with use of the kind of product being sold — thus enabling him to speak of its merits with an appearance of authority — the tone of the copy needs to be compatible with the public's perception of the writer's personality.

Advance and After-Event Shots

To mail prospects a letter that does not seek any reply — indeed, that incorporates no means even to send a reply — may seem extravagant and wasteful. Nevertheless there is sound evidence that mailing what is known as an "Advance Shot" — a letter that foreshadows the main offer, advising the recipient to look out for what is to follow — can be hugely cost-effective, particularly in the case of sweepstakes and contest offers where the copy dwells exclusively, or mainly, on the chance to win a prize that the reader will shortly receive. Typically, a strong advance can raise pull by a factor of between 25 per cent to 50 per cent.

One of the most successful advance shots that I have ever seen took the form of an assurance to readers that they had successfully passed two of the three milestones that lay along the road to becoming a winner in a prize draw. The first was selection to receive an invitation to take part, while the second was receipt of an allocation of numbers for entry in the draw.

To enhance this impression of progress along the road to riches, the mailer added to the letter which talked about these milestones, two tangible and striking tokens of the reality of the reader's chance to win, and of the possibility of imminent good fortune. The two additions to the advance letter took the form of an adhesive label personalised with the reader's name ("to be worn at the celebration prize-giving reception if you win a major prize") and a menu bearing the logo of the hotel where the reception would be held, featuring dishes from which the prize-winning guests (and their partners) would be invited to choose. Including these palpable and realistic symbols of the experience of winning added hugely to the impact of the letter and boosted response to the subsequent mailing by a substantial — and indeed almost unprecedented — figure.

Another device worth considering is a letter posted to arrive after the main mailing — a follow-up shot. This too can boost pull significantly. Whether or not it should incorporate a facility to order depends largely on the time that elapses between receipt of the main and follow-up mailings. The longer this is, the stronger the case for including a means of reply. Sometimes a so-called after-event shot follows so closely on the heels of the main mailing that there is insufficient time to exclude from the follow up those who responded to the main mailing. And sometimes what happens is that arrival of the follow-up "reactivates" its predecessor — motivating a recipient who is already half-persuaded to get off his backside and order.

Useful Extras

Useful devices worth considering for inclusion in a mailing package include what are usually known, respectively, as a "Lift Letter" and a "Jog Slip". The first is a second, much shorter, letter. This can either approach the product from a different angle to any that are part of the main letter, or it can be used to make an important additional point. It can also be used as a way to feature a testimonial or endorsement. Essentially, it is a device for giving prominence to some feature of the offer without overloading the two basic vehicles of letter and brochure. The second looks like a "Post-it" slip, and highlights one important feature of the offer.

Using a Database Creatively

Many organisations neglect the huge potential for use by skilful copywriters of information on their database. Commonly, the sole use to which this is put is in the selection of customers for appropriate offers.

While this is obviously important, its value is no greater than the potential of information about customers for use in letter copy. What customers' purchases reveal about their life-style, tastes and interests provides the copywriter with valuable knowledge which can be effectively deployed to make them further offers. Used with skill it can totally alter the customer's whole perception of a mailing — converting what might otherwise be seen as intrusive sales promotion into a genuine customer service.

When people complain about "junk mail" what they usually mean are mailings that offer them services or products that they see as irrelevant to their needs and interests.

Using information on a database a talented copywriter can present an offer in a way that demonstrates its relevance — presenting each successive offer, not as a series of one-off attempts to make a sale, but as components of a continuing relationship with customers. Very often, knowledge of what customers have purchased can be supplemented by information that they have volunteered in response to a questionnaire or survey.

But a word of warning. It is important that writers make use of this kind of information only when it has been supplied directly by the customer in the form either of a purchase, or a response to a survey. Where the information has come via some third party — as it can, for example, when a mailer has purchased someone else's list — there is an obvious danger in Mailer B revealing knowledge of a reader's relationship with Mailer A.

I once saw a company test the offer of a sewing guide to a list of people known to have bought a sewing machine. The letter, which began "As the owner of a (brand name) sewing machine you will I think be interested in our sewing guide" proved, to the mailer's astonishment, to be a total flop — pulling less than the same offer to a general list (of which an unpredictable proportion would not own any sewing machine). The reason why the letter failed was because the recipients could see no legitimate reason why the mailer (a publisher) should know that they owned a sewing machine. They had after all not bought it from the publisher, whose ostentatious display of knowledge simply aroused irritation and suspicion. In fact, had the publishers refrained from revealing this knowledge, their letter to this list would almost certainly have pulled better than its control, simply because everyone who received it possessed, in the shape of a sewing machine, what was required to benefit from buying the book.

Personalisation

So it is clearly important to show readers that any knowledge of them that the writer chooses to reveal has been legitimately come by — either by the customer's responses to market research, previous purchases — or a sensible deduction from the nature of purchases made.

For example, those who have bought a road atlas must presumably be motorists, and buyers of garden tools probably don't live in apartments.

Here then are some of the ways in which it is possible to exploit the creative potential of the database.

The first and most basic use of a database is to *personalise* the letter, with a salutation that does not say Dear Reader, Dear Friend, Dear Customer, Dear Supporter, Dear Contributor, Dear Subscriber, Dear Music Lover, Dear Motorist or use any other generalised, impersonal form of salutation. Instead it is possible to address him as:

> **Dear Mr Smith, here's an offer that I think will interest everyone at 14 Acacia Avenue.**

Next, personalisation provides an opportunity to *acknowledge the reader's individuality* by demonstrating that the organisation knows him, and values him, as an individual — not just a name on a file:

> **As one of our best customers (I see that you have been buying from us since 1991) you are naturally one of the first to be told about our latest widget.**

Another use that writers can make of the file is to signal *recognition*. You can make the reader feel as he does when he goes into a shop where he is known, where the staff are familiar with his tastes and interests:

> **We know you as a connoisseur of fine wines, with a discerning palate and a particular interest in the delicious white wines of the Loire Valley. So you will I hope welcome the chance to be among the first to sample our latest discovery . . . a crisp and fragrant Sauvignon from one of the region's most respected growers. I know that you will recognise it instantly as offering excellent value.**

Something else that you can do is use information on file to *build a relationship* with the customer. You can flatter the reader by reminding him that this current offer is not a one-off intrusion on his privacy by an aggressive marketer, but part of a continuum of *service* from a company which is interested in, and responsive to, the reader's needs.

> **It is, I see, nearly a year since you bought a dozen of our new variety of rose. And I am sure that, as spring approaches, you are looking forward with keen anticipation to enjoying a garden that is full of colour and fragrance. Bearing in mind your preference for perfume, I believe**

that you will derive much pleasure from our new introduction, Sir Les Patterson.

Information from the database can also be used to *dramatise timing*:

Looking ahead to November 30, I'd like first of all to wish you a happy birthday — and many happy returns of the day. At the same time I'd like to do something practical to make that wish come true by bringing to your notice a new kind of policy, designed especially for someone approaching retirement.

You can also use the database to *dramatise the relevance* of an offer to the reader's lifestyle:

As a motorist — worried as we all are about the soaring cost of petrol — you will, I am sure, welcome the chance to increase substantially the number of miles you get from a gallon of petrol.

Finally, you can use the database in order to dramatise the process of selection and create a *sense of privilege*:

Not all our customers are getting this opportunity. We are making this offer only to those like you who we know are interested in exploring places off the beaten track. I am sure you have happy memories of the time you spent last year in Albania. And this year you are one of the privileged few whom we are inviting to join us on a camel train to Nigeria.

It is in the opportunities that it gives copywriters to produce this kind of copy — copy that helps to build relationships with customers — that personalisation is so valuable, not in the mechanical, listless repetition of the reader's name or parts of his address: "Dear Mr Schwarzenegger" . . . "As a resident of Vermont" . . . " Money you pay into your bank in Maidstone".

What people perceive as "junk" are mailings that the recipient can see are irrelevant or indiscriminate. Simply addressing them by name does not make the thing seem like a personal letter from a company that recognises that individual's interests and concerns.

Tips on Writing Letters

- Write for an audience of one. A good sales letter is a conversation, not a broadcast or a speech.

- Make it easy for the reader to see situations in which he will benefit from having the product — and the people in his family whom it will benefit.

- Turn product features into consumer benefits.

- Use all the tricks of the trade to make your letter *readable*: subheads, underlining, capitals, quotes, short sentences and paragraphs, anecdotes, indentations, PS's, simulated handwriting, questions, exclamation marks.

- Remember the equation that readers will use to judge the value of your product:

$$\frac{\text{Benefits}}{\text{Price}} = \text{Value}$$

- Pack the letter with Benefits.

- Feature a promise, a claim or a benefit in the headline.

- Get a specific *product* or *offer* benefit into the first paragraph — if possible, into the first sentence.

- *Avoid* general statements and abstract concepts.

- Make the reader feel *privileged* to receive your offer.

- Use as often as possible throughout the letter the word "you" or one of its derivatives ("your") . . . or words where "you" is implied, either in the form of exhortation ("*try* it for seven days on approval") . . . instruction ("send no money

now") . . . or personalised fill-ins ("the whole Smith family")
. . . ("14 Acacia Road").

- Explain clearly how to order, and close by telling the reader exactly what to do.

- Check that you've made the offer absolutely clear: price, terms, premium, etc.

- Make sure that your letter gets into the right hands.

- If the reader is a customer, show that you are aware of the fact, and that you value his custom.

- Go through what you've written, and edit ruthlessly.

- Make ordering seem easy, payment painless.

- Decide at the start precisely what you wish to say, and make sure that what you write conveys the message with precision.

- Where you can do this convincingly it often pays to present a major benefit (for example, a discount, a premium or a chance to win a prize) as a *reward* for being a valued customer.

- Use a checklist of copy points, but use it sensibly. You're not landing an aircraft, you are talking to the reader.

- Make sure that your copy sounds sincere, believable and friendly.

- Make the letter typographically attractive.

CHAPTER 5

Creative Tools (2):
Brochures and Press Ads

If, as we have seen, a letter supplies the element of *personal* communication in a mailing package — the seller's contribution to a dialogue with readers — what, you might ask, is the role of a leaflet or brochure? The answer is that the brochure has two main functions to perform.

The first is *demonstration*. Next to visiting the reader with a product in your hand, the brochure — with all the opportunities it provides for graphic illustration — is the closest most direct marketers can get to the ideal situation of being able to demonstrate the product to prospective buyers. Brochures make it possible to show people what it looks like, draw attention to its outstanding features — and, where applicable, show it in action.

This is the point at which, in many cases, the brochure performs a second function — that of *explanation*. When it is thought desirable to show a product in action, to illustrate the range of uses that it has, the categories of users who will find it helpful, or the range of situations in which it will prove useful a brochure is what you need to make your point.

Be wary, though, of becoming bogged down in explanations. I have come across many instances of brochures that have foundered in a well-intentioned but misguided attempt to explain too much. The effect can be self-defeating, because the impression given to the reader comes across as one of difficulty and complexity. Instead of seeming quick and easy, using the product successfully has been made to seem laborious and difficult. What the brochure should do is demonstrate the product's uses and explain the benefits it offers. Whenever possible, try to avoid getting trapped into giving a detailed explanation of precisely how these benefits will be delivered.

Whereas in a letter the case for buying a product needs to be sequentially developed, with strong logical links within and between its component sections, a brochure does not need the same tight structure. It is much more an assemblage of components — all inter-related, but not necessarily linked sequentially. This is because illustrations encourage readers to dip and browse. While it often helps a writer to structure the brochure in sections — which can help to give the whole thing a logical coherence — this structure is not, as it would be in the case of a letter, crucial to effectiveness.

My experience has been that people seldom study brochures in the sequence planned by writers and designers. They unfold it, turn it over, reading and looking at various parts of it as the impulse moves them. The one thing that seems to govern the way readers handle a brochure is *curiosity* — the urge to keep on opening a folded piece of paper until nothing is left to unfold, and the whole thing has been reduced to what is essentially a poster with two sides.

This strong impulse to keep unfolding until no folds remain has one important implication: once past the front cover of a brochure (which is crucially important) it is probably not wise to position key passages too early in the sequence of folds; the danger — and the likelihood — is that they would be overlooked, and that the reader will simply pass them by because of the temptation to unfold.

Try to ensure that the key points occupy prime sites on either of the two surfaces that the reader is finally faced with on his two-sided poster. The designer's job is to make sure that these crucial components provide focal points for the eye to fall on, whichever side of the poster you look at.

Something else that brochures can do far more quickly and effectively than letters is to show *Who*, *When* and *Where*. Well-chosen illustrations enable readers to see at a glance the range of people whom a product or service can benefit, and the types of situation in which it will prove of value.

Given that a brochure's function is to demonstrate and explain, there are a number of features that will help it to fill this role effectively:

- *Colour*. By this I don't just mean colour in the obvious sense of colour printing. What I mean by the word is a striking presentation of a product — using words in a colourful, memorable way.

- *Drama*. A lot of brochures seem flat and lifeless; they dutifully describe and illustrate the product and list its various features in a dull, mechanical fashion. A good brochure commands the reader's interest and attention by finding some way to present the product in an arresting, striking way — and does this without straining credibility. It is a process, not of exaggeration but *enhancement* — a cosmetic rearrangement of features that heighten the product's appeal.

- *Revelation*. Telling readers something surprising or interesting that they did not already know is one proven way of stimulating appetite. It is a quick way of enabling readers to sample the product — and offers a foretaste of benefits to come.

- *Titillation*. The reverse of offering revelations, this is a process of coaxing the reader's appetite by asking questions in a way which suggests answers that will prove interesting and valuable.

- *Evocation*. If a feeling of nostalgia is likely to play a part in enhancing your product's appeal, the illustrations that are part of a brochure can play a significant part in evoking it. In this context, a single picture is worth quite a number of words. Together, words and pictures can be powerful creators of mood.

Building Blocks

There is no single correct approach to creating either a letter or a brochure. You will have to develop your own methods and techniques. However, you will find that the process can be speeded up considerably by taking advantage of the experience of others — skilled creative practitioners who have evolved their own methods . . . ways of approaching the task which work for them, and which should prove equally workable for those with less experience.

One approach that I have found consistently useful and successful in creating both letters and brochures is what I call the "building blocks" method. This involves sitting down at the outset to devise as many ways as you can think of to interest the reader in the product and the benefits of using it.

Start, I would suggest, with headlines — claims and statements — things you can say about the product in order to engage the reader's interest and attention. These are your building blocks — the components from which you will eventually assemble the completed edifice of a letter or brochure.

But don't at this early stage attempt to arrange them in a sequential pattern, or even assign them to either letter or brochure. What you are after is an assemblage — as large as you can make it — of different ways to promote the product or service that you have to sell. Once you have collected a reasonable number of these approaches to selling your product — ways of dramatising not only its uses, but also the kind of people who might find it useful . . . and the situations in which they might use it with advantage . . . you can begin to think about distributing them between letter and brochure, and the sequence in which they can be most effectively arranged. Some, you will find, can easily be illustrated; these will naturally be used in your brochure — arranged in whatever sequential pattern seems most suitable. Others, being mainly verbal rather than graphic concepts, belong more naturally in the letter. And these you will need to arrange in a more tightly structured sequential pattern than the building blocks that go into your brochure.

Often, writers make the mistake of sitting down with the intention of writing a letter or brochure straight through from beginning to end in one smooth sequential process. This can be extremely difficult. Sometimes it is hard to decide how to begin; false starts are not uncommon and often one loses creative momentum and starts to get bogged down.

But by setting out deliberately at the earliest possible stage to assemble a supply of creative building blocks you are likely to find that the whole process becomes easier and faster when you later start to piece your building blocks together to form a letter or brochure.

There are many kinds of building blocks from which you can construct your letter or brochure. One of the most important is of course *Benefits/Rewards*: a greater measure of health, wealth, personal contentment, serenity or happiness. A higher degree of personal, social or professional success. Prestige, admiration or respect. A significant diminution of some disadvantage or affliction — pain, physical, mental or emotional discomfort. A remedy for boredom in the shape of entertainment or amusement.

Other possible building blocks include:

- **Product Features**. Competitive features of the product — stronger construction, better design, lower cost, wider cover, greater durability or versatility.

- **Situations**. Where and when will the buyer be able to benefit from owning and using the product? At home, at work, at school, on the road, or when travelling abroad? In the car, the garage, the kitchen or the garden? What kind of realistic situations can you envisage in which you can credibly claim that owning the product could prove valuable or useful? If the product happens to be a practical magazine or reference work it might not be plausible to claim that the reader will always be able to turn to it for help. It might be more realistic to show that it is the *kind of information* it contains that makes its readers better prepared to cope with problems, contingencies and emergencies that seem believable.

- **People**. What categories of user might find the product relevant — parents, motorists, do-it-yourselfers, patients, students, taxpayers, employers, employees, the self-employed, householders, travellers, gardeners, cooks, etc.

- **Endorsement.**. Sometimes it is possible to include in the promotion for a product quotations from people who speak highly of it. These can be either celebrities whose names are connected with some relevant activity, and whose opinion of the product is therefore likely to carry some weight (beware of featuring testimonials from celebrities who have no obvious relevance, and who might therefore be presumed to be doing it only for the money). Or they can simply be unknown ordinary people who have used and benefited from the product, and are happy to say so (whose credibility will be much enhanced if you can give their names and addresses, or at the very least initials and post-town).

- **Terms**. The terms of the offer you are making constitute an important building block. Any attractive feature of the offer — discount, approval, instalments, guarantee, free gift, chances in a prize draw or contest — always merit emphasis and should be prominently featured.

The "building blocks" approach is particularly suited to the creation of brochures, but it can also be used just as successfully to create letters and press ads. Devote a few sentences to each of the main points that you wish to make. Then put these together in the most sensible and effective sequence, with links to provide a smooth transition from one to another in a way that seems logical and smooth.

Storyboards

One way to make the creation of a brochure easier is to think of the process in terms of "storyboards". An early stage in the production of a television commercial involves sketching out on paper a sequence of the individual frames or shots which will later be photographed in sequence to create the film: Take One — shot of a woman hailing a taxi in the street; Take Two — shows her climbing aboard the vehicle; Take Three — shows her opening her handbag — and so on through the plot's main episodes.

A brochure can be created in much the same way by arranging some of our building blocks as "takes" — a sequence of storyboards which use striking words and illustrations to promote the product.

Let's suppose for example that you are creating a brochure for a motor insurer called <u>RoadRisk</u>. Take One — (the brochure's front cover) shows two or three typical but bloodless road accident situations, each with its complement of appropriately irate/upset/contrite/embarrassed-looking models and each with a one-word caption in a starburst:

CRUNCH! THUMP! THWACK!

Above .... illustrations is the headline:

**WHEN THE CRUNCH COMES IT PAYS TO BE INSURED
WITH ROADRISK**

Take Two is a paragraph or two of copy developing the theme:

However good or experienced a driver you may be, you can still be involved in a motor accident.

Every day, the roads and motorways echo to the crunch of rending metal, the protesting squeal of tyres, the tinkle of

shattering glass. These noises signal inconvenience, distress, anxiety, <u>expense</u>. It is at such moments that it pays
to be with ROADRISK.

For a highly competitive premium (that we'll be pleased to
quote you on request) ROADRISK will give you the cover
you are required by law to have — plus one highly important
extra . . . peace of mind.

Take Three goes on to highlight the benefits of choosing this
insurer:

THESE ARE THE ADVANTAGES OF MOTOR INSURANCE WITH ROADRISK

<u>Speed</u> If the worst should happen, and you have to make a
claim, ROADRISK will deal with it efficiently and swiftly.
You won't be kept waiting for a decision while papers are
shuffled around from one department to another.

<u>Understanding</u> Here at ROADRISK there's no "us" and
"them" attitude to our policyholders. Most of us are motorists, and none of us is immune to driving accidents. We
understand the motorist's insurance needs and problems.

<u>Efficiency</u> Our nationwide network of offices — and experi-
ence gained over many years, dealing with millions of claims
— has enabled us to develop a streamlined operation. This
ensures that any claim or enquiry you make gets <u>immediate</u>
attention. We try to combine the speed and efficiency of the
electronic age with personal courteous service that makes
friends of customers.

<u>Clarity</u> Most insurance policies are difficult to read — and
even more difficult to understand. This is because they are
<u>contracts</u>, which are of course legal documents. Because
we know that most people find this legal language hard to
follow, ROADRISK have produced a "translation" in plain

English. So while the policy itself has to be in "lawyers language", you understand precisely what it means.

<u>Security</u> Established a hundred years ago, ROADRISK is one of the largest insurers in the world. Hundreds of thousands of people come to ROADRISK every year for cover against all kinds of risk — secure in the knowledge that the company's immense resources guarantee that all legitimate claims will be met.

Other possible "takes" might include a table showing the costs of typical motor repairs (all, of course, covered by RoadRisk's comprehensive policy) and another quoting premiums for typical motorists and makes of vehicle. Another possibility would be remarks from RoadRisk's policyholders, describing their satisfaction with the way their claims were handled.

Another "take" might be a photograph of a hand picking up a telephone, with copy that highlights the advantage of dealing with a company that cuts out paperwork and deals with its customers by telephone. "Phone us now, without obligation, for a quote!" would be an appropriate final message.

Although not every "take" in your brochure necessarily needs an illustration, most of them should be selected from your stock of building blocks because they provide opportunities for effective illustration.

With these concepts of building blocks and storyboards in mind, let's now take a look at ways in which they might be put into practice to produce brochures for one or two specific products.

The first is a book that sets out to explain to lay readers their legal rights and duties. This could easily sound like a rather remote and abstract proposition, whose relevance to most people's daily lives is not immediately apparent.

However, once you begin to think about the subject, the basis of a striking storyboard emerges from the fact that everybody's rights consist largely of duties owed by others. This suggests a front cover for the brochure . . . photographs of models repre-

senting various categories of people with whom we all have
some kind of relationship in law: your neighbours . . . your bank
manager . . . your employer . . . your tax inspector . . . your doctor, etc. with the following headline:

**FIND OUT WHAT ALL THESE PEOPLE OWE YOU IN THIS
IMPORTANT NEW BOOK!**

Another brochure building block: half a dozen or so case histories, each featuring some typical legal problem — but posing
rather than answering a question, explaining that these are just
a few of the many legal problems to which the book supplies
answers.

The accompanying letter echoes the theme of the brochure's front cover by offering the reader a book that explains
his rights in various capacities — as a taxpayer, consumer,
motorist, traveller, etc.

Example — Selling Health Insurance

Let's set out now to sketch out a brochure designed to promote a
health insurance company — an imaginary firm that we'll call
Healthchoice. The company offers the kind of insurance which, in
the event of illness, pays the costs of private medical treatment.
Many companies offer such insurance, and there is usually little
to choose between the terms on which they provide it. So, since
Healthchoice offers no significant competitive advantage, at the
outset we have to face the fact that none of the benefits that its
policy provides are unique, or even rare.

Analysis of motivation (see Chapter 1) reveals the main
reasons for buying this kind of insurance. It also uncovers the
characteristics of the policy offered by *Healthchoice*. Obviously the fact that they are not exclusive or unusual does not
mean that you should not mention them in your letter and
brochure. Although you are clearly precluded from claiming
that no other insurer provides them, some readers may well
assume this to be the case. And even those who do not make
this assumption will be reassured by details of the range of

cover provided by *Healthchoice*, and the nature of the serv-ice that it promises.

However, real though they are, the benefits of private medi-cal treatment and of the cover provided by *Healthchoice* will make more impact on the reader if we can find some striking or memorable way to explain them.

This is the stage at which you try to come up with conceptual building blocks from which to construct a letter and brochure. Those that lend themselves to graphic illustration are obviously more appropriate to the brochure and will provide your story-boards or "takes". Primarily verbal concepts which provide few cues or opportunities for graphics are better reserved for the letter.

One way to remind the reader of the advantages of private treatment would be to feature an illustration of someone who is obviously a patient sitting up in a hospital bed with a broad smile on her face, surrounded by flowers and smiling members of her family. This (what might be termed the "Happy Families" take), although undoubtedly a cliché, does have the advantage of implying such benefits as privacy, comfort and unrestricted visiting.

Substitute for the wife and mother somebody who is speak-ing on the telephone, with a laptop computer or calculator on the bedside table, and you are suggesting such benefits as freedom to choose a date of admission, and to keep in touch with colleagues on business issues and to combine essential work with convalescence. Let's call this the "Freedom" or "Keep in Touch" "take".

Both the Happy Families and the Freedom "takes" are ortho-dox, straightforward, perfectly valid ways of using a brochure to put across the points you wish to make. They emphasise the positive. One of the clichés of advertising practice is that points should always be made in a *positive* fashion, and that it is never wise to be negative. In my view this is nonsense. Sometimes a positive message can be communicated more effectively by featuring a negative — particularly if this can be done appropriately in an amusing or tongue-in-cheek way.

For example, everybody knows that private treatment has one big disadvantage — cost. So one possible storyboard or "take" might be a cartoon which shows a doctor examining a patient: "Where does it hurt?" the doctor's speak balloon enquiries. "In the pocket!" says the patient. The point is rammed home by a caption that conveys the reassuring message: "A *Healthchoice* policy relieves the pain of payment by meeting *all* the costs of private treatment!"

Another negative is the common perception that hospital staff view patients less as individuals than as "cases" — focusing less on the person than on the malady requiring treatment. Fairly or not, people tend to believe that private patients are recognised as individuals and enjoy more personal attention. The point might be made with an illustration that shows two nurses. The senior nurse hands the other a bedpan with the instruction "Take this to the hernia in number 4!". A caption might feature the claim: "A *Healthchoice* policy assures you of individual attention." "As a private patient you're not treated like a parcel" is the implication.

One claim that you are precluded from making is that private patients enjoy some kind of clinical advantage — that they receive better medical treatment than patients on the NHS, because this is simply not true. What is, however, perfectly legitimate is to emphasise the fact that *Healthchoice* cover enables the patient, in consultation with the family doctor, to choose the specialist best qualified to treat his problem, the hospital most conveniently placed for visits by family, colleagues and friends, and (assuming that the condition does not need urgent treatment) the date of admission best suited to his circumstances. An appropriate illustration might be a patient conferring amicably with a doctor, with a caption that declares "*Healthchoice* gives *you* the power to make decisions."

Another advantage of private health insurance is the fact that private patients do not generally have to wait long for treatment. This point can of course be made in a perfectly straightforward way by featuring the claim that, as a *Healthchoice* policyholder, you wouldn't have to join a queue. However, the claim might have more impact and be more memorable with the help of a visual such as a queue of people lining up round a hospital, or the hospital signpost idea described on page 14. If you can find some striking way to make a point, or to put across a claim, it is more likely to be noticed and remembered. (Caption: *"Healthchoice takes you off the waiting list!"*)

Incidentally, any single one of these storyboards or "takes" might provide the basis of an effective press advertisement for *Healthchoice*, possibly one that incorporates a coupon inviting readers to send for details of *Healthchoice* policies. The point that I want to put across is that effective letters and brochures are unlikely to emerge fully formed from the copywriter's head. A more fruitful approach is to think in terms of individual, conceptual building blocks from which it will later be possible to put together a letter or brochure — the second in the form of a sequence of storyboards or "takes" with strong visual components.

Other possible building blocks for the brochure could be remarks from satisfied policyholders testifying from their own experience to the benefits of *Healthchoice* cover. The brochure might also feature photographs of the kind of people whose circumstances or occupation make them particularly appreciative of the benefits of private treatment — such as the self-employed, the elderly or parents of young children.

Headlines

Headlines — both main and subsidiary — are of enormous value — particularly in creating a brochure. The main points that you want to make can be summarised in headlines, which are amplified by the body copy underneath them. Often you will find that a sequence of headlines provides you with a structure for a brochure — the headlines are, as it were, the main bones of the skeleton, which you will later be able to clothe with longer copy.

Call-Outs

Obviously in many cases you will want to show readers a picture of the product — what advertising people often refer to as a "packshot". Showing a packshot early in the sequence of "takes" that make up a brochure establishes firmly in the reader's mind the nature of your offer — reveals what it is you are talking about in the rest of the brochure.

The packshot serves several other functions. Firstly, it provides a focal point for the selling proposition; by showing the actual article that you are describing as the key to enjoyment of all the advantages and benefits you claim, you replace the abstract with the concrete.

Secondly, the design of the product may be a significant part of its appeal. Thirdly, features of its design and construction can probably be best described with the help of illustration. Often these features can best be brought to the reader's attention with the help of what are usually known as "call-outs". These are lines — either solid or dotted — which lead from the relevant portion of the illustration to an adjacent part of the brochure that provides space for words that identify the feature and explain its role.

One other function of a packshot can be to help explain the uses of a product and show the various needs and situations in which it can be of value. For example, call-outs to an illustration of a garden tool might draw attention to such features as:

Tempered toughened-steel cutting head for durability and reliability

Lightweight construction makes it easy to carry and use — even by elderly or disabled gardeners

Exclusive notched blade makes it easier to cut thick stems

Other illustrations might show situations in which the tool is useful — trimming hedges, pruning roses or shaping bushes into forms of topiary.

To sum up then, a brochure is unlike a letter in that the format does not require you to develop an argument, describe the product and dramatise its uses in a reasoned, sequential flow. The facility to use words and visual images in combination enables you to think of several, even many, possible or promising approaches to the problems of securing and holding the reader's attention, describing the product, and dramatising its uses — the benefits it offers.

As we have seen, it can be helpful to view each of these possible approaches as something like a frame in a story-board. Decide on the most appropriate visual images, the accompanying headlines and a synopsis of the copy.

Once you have assembled these "frames", the possible components of your brochure, it becomes much easier to decide if and how they can be used in combination, and to decide their sequential arrangement. Some may prove on reflection more natural components of a letter (in which case, of course, you will probably have to sacrifice the visual). Others may need to be cut or welded together. This is the stage at which your brochure begins to take shape. This shape usually has a number of components, each representing a solution to a perennial problem. The first such problem is to grab the reader's *favourable attention* in an *appropriate* fashion. So ideally the first panel of your leaflet signals the nature of the product, the main benefits it offers, or the needs and situations to which it is relevant, the main uses that it has.

The next step is to establish the nature of your proposition. This usually involves showing the product, and trying to epitomise its function.

This is followed by your *introduction* — a main headline, followed by a brief description of the product. Even if you don't actually begin this passage with the words "Here from International Widgets is . . ." you may find it helpful to bear them in mind because, in essence, this is the announcement that you're making. What follows should be your basic copy platform — the foundation of your brochure.

Next follow *demonstration, explanation, substantiation.* Demonstrate the uses of the product, explain the benefits you claim for it and substantiate those claims. *Illustrate* the kind of situations to which it is relevant and the categories of people who will find it useful.

But remember that people are short of money, time and patience. You have to make it easy for them to see at a glance what is on offer and what is in it for them — to convince them that the product is worth every cent of what is being charged for it. To do this you have to tell them — show them — with clarity and speed. They haven't got either the time or the patience to put up with tricky teasers, long drawn-out explanations, prolonged preliminaries, protracted foreplay, obscure or far-fetched introductions. Get your clothes off at the outset and show what is on offer!

To grasp and maintain your readers' interest you need to invest your proposition with elements of colour, importance, immediacy and drama — and to do this without sacrificing *credibility.* You need to present your product with conviction, enthusiasm and authority.

FOUR THINGS THE READER EXPECTS FROM YOUR BROCHURE

Identification:	What kind of product or service is on offer, and what it will do for the reader	Front cover of the brochure
Presentation:	What it is, what it looks like, and what it consists of	Packshot and product specification
Explanation:	*Raison d'être* for the product. The concept epitomised	Main headline and opening paragraphs

Demonstration:	Situations in which it will be of use; needs to which it is relevant	Salient features of the product with call-outs where appropriate.

Catalogues

If, instead of a brochure, your package includes a catalogue, your two objectives will obviously be to boost the number and value of the orders you receive. It will help you to achieve the first of these to include more than one order form with the catalogue — either for later use by a customer who orders, or for use by a friend or relative to whom the catalogue has been passed on. It can also pay to offer incentives to place orders for more than one product, or to boost the total value of an order. Either offer a particularly attractive premium for ordering more than one product, or offer entry in a contest where prizes are multiples of the aggregate value of an order.

Tips on Creating Brochures

- Show situations in which having the product can be advantageous.

- Show the categories of people (parents, gardeners, motorists, travellers, teachers, etc.) who will find the product of value.

- Feature important promises and benefits in headlines.

- Put yourself in the shoes of a door-to-door salesman as he tries to make a sale. The first thing you have to do is secure the prospect's interest, and you have a split second to do this before the door is slammed in your face. You can't of course use the traditional method of thrusting a boot in the door. What you *can* do is make sure that the front cover of your brochure is *arresting* — that it signals instantly what you have to offer, and what benefits it promises.

- Remember the functions of a brochure: demonstration, explanation.

- Remember the characteristics of good brochures: colour, drama, spectacle, news value, revelation, evocation.

- Include where you can credible celebrity endorsements or testimonials from satisfied customers or users.

- In "takes" or storyboards assemble a stock of "building blocks" and arrange those that lend themselves to illustration.

- Show not only *who* will benefit from using the product, but also *when* and *where* it will be useful.

- Provide clear focal points to catch the reader's eye, and use them to feature key claims, benefits and product features.

- Make sure that key passages don't get overlooked by the reader in his haste to unfold the brochure.

- Address all the main motivations for buying this product.

- Use call-outs to highlight significant features of the product.

- Close with a summary of benefits: "Ten reasons why it will pay you to order".

- Decide where the reader wants to be and show how your product will help him to get there.

Press Ads

While the objective remains the same — to secure an immediate order — a direct-response press ad differs from a mailing package in four significant respects.

Firstly, there is obviously much less space in which to make your pitch.

Second, your ad is unlikely to have the undivided attention of the reader; it has to compete for attention with other advertisements and, of course, editorial features.

Third, its shelf life will almost certainly be shorter. Whereas a reader may set aside for further consideration a letter or a brochure, the life of a newspaper is seldom longer than a day (magazines, of course, are longer-lived).

And finally, because it is harder to target your message, it is probable that many readers will have little or no interest in what you are trying to sell; they may find it irrelevant.

So the first thing you need to do is capture the attention of that part of the paper's readership at whom your message is aimed . . . people who might find your offer interesting and relevant.

To do this, you need to hold up an eye-catching signal, some message that instantly gets noticed by potential customers . . . that swiftly identifies the nature of your product and epitomises the benefits it offers.

Since the environment in which your ad will appear consists substantially of *news*, one approach would be to give it too a newsy feel:

NEW SAVINGS PLAN COMBINES SECURITY WITH GROWTH!

Most of the levers described in an earlier section of this book can be used in the creation of a press ad. For example:

Challenge:

DO <u>YOU</u> MAKE THESE COMMON MISTAKES IN ENGLISH?

Or:

Empowerment:

EVERYTHING YOU NEED TO KNOW TO PASS YOUR DRIVING TEST!

NOW YOU CAN GROW RHODODENDRONS EVEN ON ALKALINE SOIL!

Or:

Change:

> DO YOU STILL DO THE IRONING BY HAND?
>
> WILL YOUR PENSION BE ENOUGH FOR A
> COMFORTABLE RETIREMENT?

Or:

Novelty:

> NEW STATE-OF-THE-ART GARDENING TOOLS
> MAKE LIGHT WORK OF HEAVY SOIL

Or, of course,

Promise:

> SWIFT RELIEF FOR PAINFUL PILES!

The familiarity of this headline to ads for haemorrhoids treatments could also be used to good effect in an advertisement for private health insurance:

> SWIFTER RELIEF FROM PAINFUL PILES!

> Depending where in the country you live, you can wait as long as 12 months for an operation which isn't classed as urgent. Meanwhile, you can still be in pain — which no doubt is one reason why so many people resort to self-medication with the kind of preparations advertised with headlines like the one above.

> There is a better, safer way to secure relief. (Copy goes on to make the point about private treatment cutting the delay.)

Charities, too, can make effective use of press ads to secure gifts from sympathisers and to recruit supporters.

DOES THIS MAKE YOU ANGRY — MAKE YOU WANT TO <u>DO</u> SOMETHING?

(The illustration is a photograph of an oiled seabird)

READ HERE HOW YOU CAN HELP

If you're sickened and angered by pollution, and the harm it does to our environment and birdlife, you probably feel you want to <u>do</u> something: something to stop the poisoning of land with chemicals — the disgusting pollution of rivers and the sea with detergents and oil — in which every year, thousands of seabirds die a horrible death in a slimy film of oil.

You <u>can</u> do something — <u>now</u>. Post the coupon below with as large a sum as you feel you can afford to help the RSPB's fight against the pollution of our seas and rivers, with all the damage that it does to birdlife. The RSPB is in the forefront of the fight against pollution, and we badly need your support.

POST THIS COUPON NOW

Advertisements that aim to secure an immediate response should clearly signal what form it can take — either by featuring a coupon (with enough space provided for the reader to write his name and address with ease) or by giving a fax, telephone number, website or e-mail address.

The situation can sometimes arise where an advertiser is uncertain which of several alternative offers, ads or messages would prove the most effective. In such cases, the split-run facilities that many journals offer provide a comparatively (the comparison being with using mailing packages to test alternatives) inexpensive way of testing two or more approaches in order to identify the strongest.

Here, for example, are several different creative approaches to an ad which aims to persuade the reader to post a coupon in order to receive details of a new language course:

LEARN ANOTHER LANGUAGE "ON LOCATION" IN YOUR HOME

Here's a totally new, up-to-date approach to learning another language easily and quickly. It uses not only printed and audio material, but <u>videos</u> shot on location in France, Spain, Italy and Germany — featuring nationals of these countries in real-life situations of the kind that you are likely to find yourself in when you go abroad.

———————

ONE FORM OF TRAVEL INSURANCE THAT NO TRAVEL AGENT OFFERS: INSURANCE AGAINST DISAPPOINTMENT!

Of all the risks of foreign travel, the commonest is <u>disappointment</u> — the failure of a holiday or business trip caused by inability to speak the language of the country that you visit. Without that ability you are tongue-tied, dependent on pantomime gestures, Pidgin English or appeals for help to a passing local who happens to speak English.

———————

REMEMBER HOW EASILY YOU LEARNED JOINED-UP WRITING?

Here's a new way to master joined-up speech in French, Spanish, German or Italian!

"Bonjour" . . . "Prego" . . . "Bitte" . . . "Por favor" . . . Most of us can manage a few halting words or phrases in a foreign language. Far more happily placed are those who have taken the trouble to pick up enough of the language of the countries that they visit on holiday or business to be able to converse with the nationals in their own language.

If you'd like to move on to joined-up speech in any of these languages, send now etc, etc.

"La Plume De Ma Tante Est Dans La Poche Du Jardinier . . ."

AT LAST, A LANGUAGE COURSE THAT HAS
THROWN OUT "THE PEN OF MY AUNT"!

Most of us are familiar with the stilted clichés of conventional, old-fashioned language courses — bizarrely preoccupied as so many are with artificial and unrealistic situations.

Now there is a totally new, up-to-date approach to learning a foreign language easily and quickly, etc. etc.

Always Wanted To Be Able To Speak Another Language?

HERE'S A QUICK, EASY AND ENJOYABLE WAY TO
CRASH THE LANGUAGE BARRIER

If you were setting out to create a brochure for this course, you would probably be able to incorporate more than one of these approaches. But in the case of a press ad there is only room for one of them, and split-run testing offers a means of establishing which is most effective.

Chapter 6

Creative Tools (3):
The Internet, TV, Radio and Telephone

Although this is the only chapter devoted specifically to the subject of writing copy for the electronic media — TV, radio, telephone and the Internet — in truth the advice in much of the book can provide help for writing for these relatively new media. For the fact is that the principles, techniques and skills of writing good copy are much the same in every medium; anyone who really understands and masters them should be capable of adapting and applying them intelligently to the opportunities and limitations of other media.

Something else that should be recognised is that close parallels exist between the longer-established print advertising media and various aspects of the Internet. Banners are a bit like the posters that line the boundaries of sports grounds, with the important difference that they tell viewers where to go for further details. It is also possible to ensure that these banners are placed only on web pages that are most likely to be seen by people with relevant needs and interests. In this respect, selling on the Internet can be likened to selling through classified ads, most of which are seen only by people whose interests are relevant to the products and services on offer. Advertisements on websites have much in common with space ads in the press, and many of the proven techniques for writing good direct mail copy are just as effective when the words are to be e-mailed.

A lot of copy written for e-mail and advertisements on web-sites betrays a common misconception: this is that because the Internet is still a young, developing medium which is growing fast and exponentially, people's motives for buying — and the techniques for persuading them to do so — must necessarily be different from those that have been evident for many years in long-established media.

This is in my view a delusion. Human nature does not change simply because methods of communication do. The prospect who has just opened his e-mail, or clicked onto a website, is impelled by exactly the same motivations — driven by the same desires, fears and ambitions — as the individual reading a press ad, watching television, listening to the radio or opening a mail shot. Indeed he is the same person. He has not suddenly become some strange new kind of animal, speaking a different language, simply because he is sitting in front of a computer risking eye strain by looking at a flickering screen, Repetitive Stress Injury by constant pounding of the keyboard, or near-terminal boredom by scrolling what sometimes looks like the interminable text of a web page.

Internet users do, however, for as long as they are sitting in front of the screen, have in common certain characteristics and attitudes that it is wise to take into account.

They are, to start with, likely to be in a hurry; they have neither the time nor the patience to pay attention to wordy, fanciful or complex messages that fail to capture their interest on sight, and quickly follow through with a promise of real benefits. They will, too, be sceptical of boastful ads which lack relevance and credibility.

As in other media, the competition for attention is fierce and comes not only from other marketers, but also from the limitless range of informative and entertaining websites. It is usually in search of *information* of some kind that people sit down in the first place to surf the net, and they are unlikely to be distracted or diverted from their search by any message that they perceive as irrelevant to their needs, problems or ambitions, or as inappropriate to their lifestyle.

In the matter of format, tone and content every medium of communication evolves its own conventions. Those of the press ad, letter and brochure — as well as of radio and TV ads — are now fairly well established. In the case of the Internet, however, they are still evolving. Unsurprisingly in such a young medium, one observable feature of many messages is a certain *informality* of tone, along with a briskness and brevity of language that has something in common with telegraphic messages sent by people who are pressed for space and time.

Immediacy

The Internet has one significant feature which operates to the marketer's advantage: it has an *immediacy* that generates a sense of *urgency* which are both helpful to the copywriter in propelling prospects into action.

There is, however, a downside. Like those who advertise in other media, Internet users have evolved a jargon of their own. Two words in particular serve as a warning to the copy-writer: junk mail has its e-mail counterpart in the form of what are known as "Spams" — offers that recipients perceive as unwanted, intrusive, uninteresting and irrelevant. And whereas junk mail just gets pitched straight into the waste bin, the quality of immediacy just mentioned tends to generate an actively hostile response from recipients of "Spams" who react angrily with abusive replies in the form of what have come to be known as "Flames".

These characteristics of urgency and immediacy make it all the more important to signal at the outset the relevance of offers made by e-mail and to highlight unmistakably the benefits they promise.

The Internet is a curious hybrid. Although a visual, electronic medium which can make effective use of graphics, it also leans heavily on the printed word — albeit in a format that is not the easiest to read. Tightly packed words on a flickering screen add up to a formula for eye strain. So it is imperative to use every possible device to make your message, not only interesting, but also easy to read.

Useful devices for enhancing legibility include:

• Generous use of white space

• Wide margins

• Short sentences

• Short paragraphs

• Short lines (each, ideally, of not more than 60 characters).

Other devices for making copy more readable and effective include using headlines and subheads that are built around punchy, forceful words, particularly action verbs which promise benefits:

Lose *pounds in days . . .*

Speak *French fluently . . .*

Command *your audience's attention and respect*

In the interests of maintaining *credibility* and *authority* steer well clear of such tacky, hucksterish practices as printing every other word in capitals, or — when talking about making (or saving) large amounts of money — printing multiple pound or dollar signs ("add ££££s to your profits! . . . Save $$$$s within days!").

Earlier we noted that a certain informality of language is one of the emerging characteristics of Internet copy. But let's be clear what is meant by informality — or rather a tone of voice which, though informal, is also *acceptable* and *appropriate*, both to the nature of the product, and to the kind of people who make up your target market. Informality is fine in the sense of copy that is neither pompous nor stilted, but straightforward and relaxed in a way that echoes the patterns of speech. "Write as you speak" is a useful maxim whatever the medium in which your copy will appear. But it is particularly good advice to follow if you are writing copy for the Internet.

It is equally important to be clear what informality does *not* mean. It does not mean *wacky*. A lot of the copy one finds in e-mails and on websites seems to be couched in the linguistic counterpart of a baseball cap worn back to front — it betrays a delusion that people will like you better if you come across as funky and totally relaxed. Too often, though, what are relaxed are the rules of literacy and grammar. Informality does not mean illiteracy. Misspellings and a poor grasp of grammar are no more acceptable on the Internet than in any other medium. On the contrary, they have a way of leaping off the screen to undermine the authority and credibility of the copy. Instead of the effect presumably intended of suggesting that International Widgets are a bunch of regular cool guys with whom it is fun to do business, sloppy English, multiple misspellings and a poor grasp of grammar — together with inattentive proof reading — all strongly suggest that you would be dealing with a bunch of slobs.

Some of the prevalent "wackiness" stems from another delusion which is that the best way to get noticed is to be outrageous. This curious belief once spawned such aberrations as press ads printed upside down, or TV ads built around some feeble joke that fast becomes more irritating with each successive viewing. The fact is, of course, that the key to being favourably noticed is to approach the people who make up your target market with relevant offers that hold out, in a credible way, the realistic prospect of worthwhile benefits.

It cannot be too strongly or too often emphasised that the process of coaxing people to part with their hard-earned money in exchange for your product or service is primarily a matter of persuasively-presented information. If such a message can be entertaining too, without sacrificing credibility, so much the better. But we are none of us in the entertainment business and people did not open your e-mail or visit your website in search of laughs. If your ad makes them laugh it may well be because it strikes them as the work of a buffoon!

Much of the Internet's potential as a tool for marketing lies as much in the technical as in the creative area, with devices such as "cookies" providing opportunities to track the behaviour of consumers on the Internet . . . what they buy, which websites and pages they visit, where they go for information and so on. In such ways marketers can amass a wealth of commercially valuable information about the buying habits, tastes and interests of consumers.

Scope for Personalisation

This kind of information is valuable not only for selection purposes, making it possible to target prospects with precision and ensure that the offers they receive are relevant and appropriate. It can also be used by writers to present offers made by e-mail as being more in the nature of a service to the customer than a piece of aggressive sales promotion. Amazon.com is one e-marketer who makes skilful and effective use of information about the tastes and interests of their customers that they acquire — quite legitimately — in the course of doing business with them. They keep in contact by regularly e-mailing newsletters with relevant information about the titles they can offer which are demonstrably relevant to the reader's range of interests. One of the smartest and most successful users of the Internet, Amazon know very well the value of positioning what is essentially sales promotion as a *service* — something that customers appreciate because they perceive the information they are sent as relevant and interesting. Cleverly written copy that makes skilful use of the opportunities to personalise approaches by e-mail can minimise the risk of their being perceived as "Spams" by the people who receive them.

Using Incentives on the Net

It strikes me that many advertisers on the Internet are failing to make use of a valuable tool for securing attention and response in the shape of *incentives* — devices of proven effectiveness described in Chapter 5 on Incentives. These are just as relevant to advertising on the Internet as they are when using other media. Sweepstakes (prize draws) and Premiums (free gifts) in particular might, if featured in a banner, substantially boost the number of those motivated to click on to a website or home page for details of the product or service on offer *and* of how to claim the incentive.

> **Garden lovers! — see what's new in plants, materials and tools. For free full-colour catalogue, and your chance to win £50,000 in our free-to-enter draw, visit the Pink Hydrangea website on . . .**

> **Best prices on new Volvos and the best current deal on your current model. For details and chance to win £5,000 in our free-entry prize draw, visit the Acme Cars website on . . .**

A banner ad featuring an incentive can be placed on affinity websites and on menus where it is likely to be seen only by people in the market for what you are selling. For example, in the case of a nursery a banner could be planted in the websites of horticultural institutions, gardens to visit, seed suppliers, suppliers of garden tools and equipment, landscape gardeners and garden designers, etc:

> **See what's new in the garden and win up to £5,000 in our free-to-enter draw! Visit the Pink Hydrangea website on . . .**

> **Quality cars at low, direct-sale prices — plus free AA membership! For details, click on now to . . .**

> **Low-cost private medical treatment for yourself and your dependants — for free personal quotation without obligation and a chance to win up to £5,000 in a free-entry prize draw see the Healthchoice website on . . .**

Sweepstakes

Sweepstakes have two unique advantages as what might be described as "mousetraps" — devices for luring people to your ad or website, and once there motivating them to respond. One is a powerful incentive to respond, in the shape of a chance to win a valuable and attractive prize — a car, a holiday or a substantial sum of money.

The second advantage springs from a quirk of human nature referred to again in the chapter on "Sweepstakes and Contests". The great majority of sweepstakes entrants mistakenly believe that their chance of winning will be significantly better if they respond in a way they imagine the sweepstakes operator would prefer — that is to say, by buying the product, sending for details, seeking a personal quotation, or whatever. As we see in that chapter there is, in many jurisdictions, a legal requirement that all sweepstakes entrants should have an equal chance to win, whether or not they spend any money with the operator. But the fact is that no matter how clearly you explain that all entrants have exactly the same chance of winning, most people simply don't believe you. Fortunately for sweepstakes users, consumers persist in the conviction that, like the creatures in George Orwell's *Animal Farm*, "all animals are equal, but some are more equal than others", and that in order to enjoy the fullest measure of equality it is necessary to respond to sweepstakes offers in a way that the operator is likely to prefer.

This fact has obvious implications for offers made on the Internet by marketers who wish to secure an "opt-in", i.e. the permission of responders to record personal details with a view to making further individual approaches in the future. Obviously an opt-in greatly increases the value of a response to any e-mail approach by enabling you to build your database. So it pays to encourage the belief that opting-in will give responders a better chance to win.

Tips on Writing for the Internet

- Embody in your banners a crisply-worded benefit headline in order to lure searchers and browsers to your website.

- Feature prominently, beginning with the headline, the *benefits* of what you have to offer — and *prioritise* these so that the strongest come first.

- Treat competitive features of your product, offer or service in just the same way: put the most compelling up front.

- Design your website in such a way that every page is headed by a benefit or star product feature.

- Make your copy easy on the reader's eye. Keep words, sentences, lines and paragraphs short. Break the copy up with plenty of headlines and subheads. Wide margins and plenty of white space enhance readability. Remember that long lines and too many capitalized words make copy more difficult to scan; so too do long, scrolling texts.

- Target prospects who contacted you, thereby providing you with an excellent reason to get back to them in a way that positions your approach as a *service*.

- Steer clear of Spams — indiscriminate e-mailing of solicitations that recipients are likely to find of no interest or irrelevant (in other words, electronic junk mail).

- Take care to use a tone of voice that is appropriate to your product and the kind of people who make up your target market. The kind of wacky, unbuttoned approach that might appeal to teenage music buyers is unlikely to convince an older prospect of the merits of a new financial service.

- Set your "mousetraps" carefully. Browsers who are speeding along the "information superhighway" are only likely to pause long enough to read your message if you can capture their attention with a striking promise of a worthwhile benefit.

- Steer clear of tricky, fanciful copy. Cute or whimsical approaches of the kind that might (just *might!*) be acceptable or effective in a direct mail package or print advertisement will go down like a lead balloon in e-mail or on a website. The Internet is above all a medium to which people turn for *information*, which is most acceptable when straightforwardly presented. If the prospect had been looking for a laugh he would have clicked on to a chat room or some other site that promised entertainment.

- Feature prominent calls to action. Tell prospects how you want them to respond, and give them contact details — fax and telephone numbers, e-mail address etc.

- Wherever possible provide some extra incentive to respond and to do so swiftly . . . for example, free sweepstakes entry, free information, free gift.

Copywriting for the TV, Radio and the Telephone

Once again the principles, techniques and strategies of selling described throughout this book are just as relevant to telephone selling and to writing advertisements for TV and radio that are directed to securing an immediate response. There is, however, one major difference between these three media and direct mail, press ads and the Internet. The difference is that whereas contact with selling messages in the three latter media is largely voluntary, TV and radio ads force themselves on the attention. Often they interrupt an activity that the listener or viewer is enjoying, and are therefore resented as an irrelevant, unwanted intrusion. Few people, unless they are paid to do so, would volunteer to watch or listen to an ad, a fact that suggests that it would be smart for advertisers to bear in mind that they are not present in the prospect's home as it were, by invitation; their presence is uninvited and may well be resented. So if you are writing for this kind of audience it will pay you to remember that you are in the prospect's home on sufferance, and to behave in a way that distinguishes a guest from an intruder — in other words with courtesy and a certain amount of dignity.

It is like hearing the doorbell ring when you are watching the news or listening to music. The intrusion may compel attention, but it is unlikely to be welcome. So if what you are trying to do is make a sale, it would be wise to do what you can at the outset to disarm your prospect and put him in a more receptive mood.

How can you do this in the limited time available? The answer is by presenting yourself in a favourable light, which means in the first place by addressing your prospects politely, and secondly by coming swiftly to the point and making abundantly clear the relevance of your product.

Remember Verdi and his opera AIDA — because here, too, you have just a few seconds to capture *Attention*, kindle *Interest*, stimulate *Desire* and prompt immediate *Action*.

So you need to do four things quickly:

1. Hold up some signal that instantly captures the attention of your prospect.

2. Say who you are and what you have to offer

3. Quickly run through the major benefits.

4. Tell people how to order.

> **When one of the family is ill, it's frustrating and worrying to have to join a waiting list for treatment.**
>
> **You don't have to queue for any treatment that you need. A new low-cost policy from Healthchoice provides full insurance at a price you can afford against the costs of private treatment in the hospital of your choice by the specialist that your GP recommends.**
>
> **For details and a personal quotation, free of obligation call us now (contact details).**

Nobody wrote more tuneful music than Tchaikovsky. Now 60 of the best-loved pieces by the world's favourite composer — given stunning performances by top-flight orchestras — are gathered in a fine new collection — available on two CDs exclusively from Maestro-Music. To order yours, call now (contact instructions).

"You can lose weight safely, easily and quickly. A new book from Acme Publishers reveals the secrets of top dieticians . . . brings you, for only $20, the professional tips, expert advice and proven weight-loss programs for which delighted clients gladly pay hundreds of dollars. Follow their recipes and instructions and success is guaranteed, or your money back.

If you can't wait to lose weight send for your copy now (contact details)."

Common to all these examples is a straightforward presentation of information that is clearly relevant to the interests, needs or problems of significant numbers of people. Each ad targets one of these interest groups with a message framed to capture their attention and clearly signpost the way to securing the promised benefits.

Sometimes an advertiser is obliged by the provisions of legislation or a code of practice to include in the ad either a warning (for example, that share values can go down as well as up) or details of certain conditions on which the offer is made ("terms and conditions apply", "subject to financial status") and so on. These spoken equivalents of "small print" can even in extreme cases occupy more time than the selling messages that preceded them, and — positioned as they are at the end of the ad — they can undermine it totally.

If your ad is subject to such constraints, take care to use the minimum permissible number of words, and to include a clear call to action along with full order instructions. Try to end on a *positive* note.

Telephone Selling

In the case of radio and TV ads, you — the writer — are in full and exclusive control of the script. With telephone selling it is different: the other person on the line hasn't got the script, and may well have ideas of his own about the course that he wants the conversation to take. It is therefore unwise to give sales people too rigid and inflexible a script: it is clearly more realistic to provide them with an outline of the product (or service) benefits or features that they are expected to mention, and allow them the freedom to improvise, mentioning these features in conversation as appropriate opportunities occur.

Here is such an outline of the points to be made in the course of telephone conversation between a member of the sales force, and the holder of a household contents policy.

> **Good evening Mr Smith, Brian here from Acme Insurance (your household contents insurer).**
>
> **I have been asked to bring you up to date on some valuable extras that you can have added to the cover your current policy provides.**

Points to make where appropriate in the course of conversation:

Low extra cost:

> **Just a small addition of £x to the current premium secures all these extra benefits:**

Extra benefits include:

> **Up to £x,000 Householder's Liability insurance covers you against the cost of any successful claim made by anybody who suffers accidental injury while on a visit to your premises, or by anything (such as a loose tile) that falls off your property.**
> **Last year alone more than £x,000,000 was paid out by insurers to successful claimants in compensation for injury or damage suffered in this way.**

<u>Extended cover</u> for valuables that you take outside the home. At present, your policy only covers a limited number of specific valuables that are lost or stolen while outside your home. Now you can make sure that all your treasures are fully covered while outside your home — for example, while you are away on holiday, or on a visit to a restaurant or shop — even if they are stolen from your car.

<u>Legal advice hotline</u>. If, while this policy is in force, you should have a legal problem that involves either your home or its contents, you can telephone free for expert advice from a lawyer who specialises in this field. For example, if a builder proves to have botched work done for you, a telephone call will put you instantly in touch with a lawyer who will explain your rights and advise you what to do.

<u>Reason for prompt action</u>. As I said, the cost of these extra benefits is small — in your case, just £x. And if you'd like to agree the small extra premium now, the additional cover will come into force right away — you won't have to wait until the renewal date of your policy.

I wouldn't want you to miss out on these important extra benefits. Thank you for taking the time to talk to me. Is there anything else you'd like to ask me while you are still on the line?

With radio, TV and telephone selling it pays to bear in mind the kind of demeanour and behaviour that most people find objectionable in a visitor. You do not, for example, expect to open the door or pick up the telephone and find yourself faced by some aggressive loudmouth, shouting and guffawing, and clearly intent on trying to sell you something you don't want. Such approaches are no more acceptable when the intrusion is made via a loudspeaker or telephone line.

Bear in mind that famous piece of advice: "Speak softly, and carry a big stick" — the stick in this case being replaced by a carrot!

Chapter 7

Sweepstakes, Contests, Gifts and Other Incentives

The motivation to buy your product can spring from either of two sources. One is the product itself: its various distinctive features and the benefits these offer to the owner — coupled with the skilful way that you present them — have kindled in your prospect a desire to possess it.

But this may not be enough. The impulse to buy can be ephemeral and fragile, and may well not survive long enough to generate an order. This is a risk that many advertisers *have to* take — the danger that the fuse lit by a TV or press advertisement may fizzle out before the prospect has an opportunity to purchase.

The direct marketer does not need to take that risk. He can supply prospects with the means to release the impulse to buy *immediately*, and what is more provide an incentive to do so in the shape of some attractive extra benefit. This might be a premium (a free gift), the chance to win a prize in a sweepstakes or a contest — or possibly a discount. Such incentives reduce substantially the delay between ignition of the fuse and the action that you seek — which is of course an order.

Incentives usually work better if you make them *conditional* — the condition being a *prompt* order. Ideally, you should specify a deadline . . . 5, 10 days or whatever. Pick a period short enough to generate swift action, but not so short that you miss getting orders from people who for some reason did not make immediate contact with your offer, and therefore may fear that they might have missed the bus.

Of course, once an impulse to purchase has been generated, the quickest and easiest way to release it is to pick up a telephone or use the internet or a fax machine. A powerful incentive package might, for example, include one or more of the following components:

- The facility to order by telephone, e-mail or fax

- The chance to win a prize in a sweepstakes or contest

- A separate prize or bonus conditional on prompt response

- The offer of a free gift conditional on placing a prompt order

- A discount.

Let's take a closer look at each of the incentives:

Sweepstakes and Contests

While the principal objective is naturally always to secure an order, there is often a significant secondary aim. This is simply to get a reply — *any* reply, positive or negative. This is because the more people you can motivate to reply, the greater the number of orders you'll receive. So it nearly always pays to ask for a response to your offer, whatever form it takes. Of course it helps to give a reason ("because it will help us to plan production" or "because we have only a limited number of places to offer, and it would help us to know if the one held for you can be released to someone else").

The best way to secure replies is to make it plain to readers that it is in their own interests to respond. And the classic device for doing this is to offer all who respond the chance to win a valuable prize — in other words, entry in a sweepstakes or a contest.

In some jurisdictions, including the UK and the US, it is not permissible to offer sweepstakes entry only to those who buy your product. Nor is it legal to discriminate between positive and negative responders by, for example, offering extra sweepstakes chances or extra sweepstakes prizes to those who buy your product.

Why, then, does it pay to use sweepstakes if those who do not order have to be permitted to take part? There are in fact two reasons, the first of which has already been mentioned: the more replies you can generate, the more orders you will receive. And few things stimulate response more effectively than sweepstakes. The second reason why sweepstakes generate more orders is because, human nature being what it is, people don't believe it when you tell them that the only condition of entry is *response*. Most of them suspect that negative responses will be consigned to the incinerator. They cling suspiciously to the belief that placing an order gives a better chance to win.

This artificial stimulant to positive response might be expected to produce inferior performance in the shape of either high rejections or poor payments. These are the typical penalties for over-stimulating orders, either by over-selling the product, or by applying too many extraneous pressures to reply. There is, however, a reason why this is less likely to happen with a sweepstakes. So long as people think that they are still in with a chance to win one of the prizes (a fact of which it is only sensible to remind them when you send your bill) they will not wish to — as many imagine — jeopardise their chances by doing anything that might give offence to the sweepstakes promoter, such as rejecting the product or failing to pay.

It was mentioned earlier that negative responders have to be offered equal chances in the sweepstakes. However, equal chances are not the same as equal treatment. There are two things that can be legitimately done to tilt the scales in favour of a positive response. One is to make the method of entering the sweepstakes more difficult and onerous for those who do not order — for example, by having to find their own envelope and write in with their name and address. This is what many manufacturers of packaged goods do when they make use of sweepstakes to help sell their products in retail outlets. All the razzmatazz is on the label or package, and the easiest way to take part is to buy the product. But if your eyesight is good, and you are diligent enough to search for it, you are likely to find buried somewhere in the small print a legal incantation on these lines:

> **No purchase necessary. If you do not wish to buy, but want to take part in the sweepstakes, write to us with a note of your name and address.**

The second device for encouraging a positive response is to offer those who place an order the chance to win an extra prize. To make this legal, the extra prize needs to be one that is awarded, not to an entrant in the sweepstakes, but to someone who enters a *contest* that is open exclusively to buyers.

Types of Sweepstakes

If you choose a sweepstakes as your incentive, you have a choice between two forms of draw: a *pre-draw* or a *post-draw*. The first takes place *before* the mailing is sent out; the second form of draw takes place *after* the mailing, when all the people who wish to enter have sent back replies to your offer. They do not of course *need* to be allotted numbers — they can simply enter their names. The purpose of sending people numbers to enter in the draw is simply to dramatise the fact that they have several chances to win.

Pre-Draws

The main advantage of a pre-draw is the opportunity it provides to remind the reader that failure to reply — not sending back for checking the number that could already have drawn a valuable prize — could be tantamount to throwing money away. Returning numbers in a draw that has already taken place is a bit like taking an antique along for valuation: while it is probably worth nothing, there remains a genuine possibility that it might — just might — be worth a lot of money. And since a "valuation" costs nothing, it would be foolish not to seize the opportunity.

Here are two examples of copy that exploits some of the potential of a pre-draw:

Example 1

Something you hold in your hand right now could turn out to be worth a cool £50,000.

Week after week on television, the Antiques Road Show provides the cheering spectacle of people learning that something that they might have thought of negligible value was actually worth a small fortune.

Now the same could be about to happen to you. Return your prize draw entry form for "valuation" and any of the numbers on it could turn out to be worth £50,000.

You see, Mr Smith, yours are among the numbers that we have entered in a draw that has already taken place. All the numbers entered — including, of course, the one that has drawn £50,000 — are being distributed at random with offers of our products.

This means, since six of them have been allocated exclusively to you, that you could at this moment be holding the winning number in your hand.

There is only one way to find out if one of your numbers is already worth £50,000: return them all to us for "valuation" <u>now</u>.

Example 2

You don't need to have cash in hand to make the mistake of throwing money away.

Right now there could be money — £50,000 — waiting in the bank for you. And I don't want you to make the mistake of throwing it away.

£50,000 is the valuable prize in a draw that has already taken place — the prize that is waiting now for the holder of the winning number.

That person could be you! Only if you send your number back for checking will we know if it's the winner. If you don't send it back you could literally be throwing away £50,000.

Post-Draws

There is no such powerful hook in the case of a draw that has yet to take place, where the reader simply sends back a request (which may or may not involve sending back numbers) to be entered in a draw. As already explained, the only advantage of numbers is to dramatise multiple chances in the case where a computerised draw has been set up which provides each entrant with more than a single chance to win.

Here are two examples of copy being used — this time — to offer readers chances in a post-draw:

Example 1

Here's a chance for you to make — without paying or risking a penny — an instant, tax-free capital gain of £100,000.

Imagine the pleasure of receiving instantly, in one fell swoop, a sum that most of us would be lucky to build up in a lifetime — from hard-earned salary or wages, and painfully-accumulated savings.

There are of course other ways in which you might come by such a windfall. But most of them cost money and involve taking a risk.

In total contrast, your chances to share in our £250,000 prize draw payout cost you nothing and involve no risk or obligation.

Why miss such an opportunity? £100,000 may not be a fortune by national lottery standards; it would not be enough to turn your life upside down, or bring you sacks of begging letters. But it's more than enough to make a very pleasant difference to your own and your family's standard of living.

A good enough reason, surely, to send in your prize draw entry <u>now</u>.

Example 2

All the people who have won in our prize draws (so far 50,000 of them have shared more than £2 million!) achieved their big win in three stages. And I'm happy to say that you have already completed two of them. Your se- lection to receive an invitation to take part saw you safely through the first stage of our latest draw, in which 100 winners will be sharing £250,000. And now with the re- ceipt of six numbers for entry in the third and final stage, you have now completed the second.

But before we can pay out the £250,000 that is waiting for the winners there is one last thing that you must do for your chance to be among them: send in the numbers on your entry form so that we can enter them for you in the third and final stage.

That's all you need to do for your chance to be on that long list of winners!

Contests

Along with sweepstakes, contests are another classic direct marketing incentive. And in certain circumstances they can be just as effective as sweepstakes, particularly as a contest pro- vides creative opportunities that are not available in the case of sweepstakes.

The first, as already explained, is the opportunity to discriminate in favour of those who place an order. In the case of contests, it is perfectly permissible and legal to lay down conditions of entry, for example by restricting chances to win to those who buy your product, or who are already customers. If you were to offer sweepstakes entry only to those who become — or who already are — your customers, the law would say that they had in effect "bought" their chance to win by purchasing your products.

There is no such risk with a contest. You can stipulate any conditions you wish that work to your advantage. The only legal requirement is that any prizes you offer are awarded solely on the basis of entrants' skill and judgement. This means of course that you have to supply them with an entry form — or at least make it possible for them to create their own, by for example listing "in order of importance" features of your product or the uses to which it is put. A common type of contest entry takes the form of a photograph of some ball game, from which the ball has been removed. This makes possible an invitation to participants to exercise their skill and judgement to indicate the precise position of the missing ball, using such clues as the positions of the players and the direction of their gaze.

Most contest entry forms that one comes across seem unoriginal and boring, but there is a good reason why this should be so. Completing an entry form costs effort, and by and large most people are lazy. They do not want to spend hours composing a limerick, or writing an essay about their reasons for wishing to take a holiday in Kathmandu. Bored with endless spot-the-ball forms, creative people often make the mistake of trying to devise an entry form that will be "fun" to complete. The effort is usually misguided. People do not regard filling in contest entry forms as "fun", any more than filling in a football pool coupon or a lottery ticket is fun. What they want is to get the whole tedious process over quickly; the fun lies in winning, not in the process of entry.

Spot-the-missing-ball entry forms have two advantages: arguably success does involve a substantial element of skill and judgement — a fact to which you can, as a form of legal "scarecrow", get an expert who will serve on the judging panel to testify. Nevertheless, although those who may wish to do so are free to spend hours exercising skill and judgement in an attempt to locate the missing ball, the majority of much lazier entrants can if they so choose pick at random with a pin the location of the missing ball. They may not stand much chance of success, but the decision is their own. In other words, people can enter at any level they prefer.

You need to take care to ensure that skill and judgement are genuinely needed to succeed. Although many promoters use the phrase simply as an incantation, there is always the risk of a prosecution mounted on the allegation that, since no real skill and judgement are involved, the scheme is not a contest but an illegal lottery.

The other advantage of a contest to a copywriter are the opportunities it provides for "recognition" and "favouritism" copy. "As a gold card holder, you are cordially invited to take part in a contest open exclusively to our account customers."

Contests are a more flexible form of incentive than sweepstakes because of the opportunities they provide to discriminate in favour of those who buy your products. They have however two disadvantages. Not only must participants be supplied with entry forms; you have also to set up machinery for judging every entry. You must also recognise that the majority of people are lethargic. Entering contests requires an effort, however minimal. What is more, most people make no distinction between the two kinds of prize scheme — and see no difference between sweepstakes and contests. They may therefore be puzzled and irritated when they receive — as they have to — a contest entry form. They would much rather just send off a ticket for free entry in a sweepstakes and sit back to await the good news that they have effortlessly won a pot of money.

The necessity to keep supplying entry forms makes contests unsuitable for continual, repeated use on the same lists. With sweepstakes on the other hand you can keep approaching the same lists with the same incentive.

Contests present fewer legal problems. You can if you wish make entry conditional on order. You can even make a charge for entry — or offer free entry to buyers, and charge non-buyers for the privilege of entry. And invitations to take part in a contest can be presented as a "perk" for customers — a reward for the purchases that they have made from you in the past. The only legal pitfall is that of allowing too many entries in the same contest. If you give entrants too many chances to win, you risk the accusation that winning hinges more on chance than skill, and so that the scheme is in fact a lottery.

If you choose a prize draw as your incentive, it pays to give careful thought to your prize list. Aim for a reasonable balance between quantity and quality — between a few large, attractive prizes and a lot of smaller value. Cash is infinitely flexible and versatile — obviously winners can spend it in any way they choose. Merchandise prizes, on the other hand, are easier to illustrate and dramatise — for example with metal car keys or simulated airline tickets — both among the classic returnable action devices that dramatise chances to win.

If you are lucky, and mailing in large numbers, you may be able to persuade suppliers to let you have prizes free of charge, or at a discount, in return for the free publicity that your promotion would provide for them.

It is advisable to steer clear of the kind of prize which — while it might appeal strongly to some — would have no attractions whatever for a significant proportion of people. Most grandparents don't want to win a speedboat or a hang-gliding holiday. Humdrum and unimaginative though they might seem, the most attractive prizes are those which are universally acceptable — such as cash, cars and holidays. The same, incidentally, is true — albeit at much lower values — of premiums. A soil-testing kit may not sound like a gift to set the pulses racing. But if your product is being sold to gardeners, such a premium would be of use and value to just about anyone who might buy it. A good premium has three characteristics: it should be universally attractive, preferably exclusive and ideally have a quality of "cuteness".

Legal Considerations

The legal distinction between sweepstakes and contests is not just academic. Depending on the nature of your business, it can have important implications for the effectiveness of your promotion.

Suppose for example that a building society or bank is looking for an incentive that will persuade potential customers to open an account, and at the same time encourage current customers to increase the size of their deposits. The type of incentive that comes most readily to mind is a prize draw. But unless this, presumably highly respectable, institution is prepared to run the risk of prosecution, a prize draw is ruled out on legal grounds. The law on illegal lotteries prohibits making chances in a draw conditional on "contribution" or "consideration", which effectively rules out not only any kind of purchase, but also depositing money with the institution — or indeed on increasing the size of funds already held.

However, provided it can be shown that the prizes offered will be awarded solely on the basis of "skill and judgement" displayed by entrants, it would be entirely legal to make entry to a *contest* conditional, either on becoming a customer, or on increasing the size of a deposit.

And since the marketer's objective is to attract not only customers but funds, it would obviously be sensible to relate the condition to the aim — which is to maximise the size of funds held on deposit.

Why not then offer prizes which are all (subject of course to a specified limit on the amount of each prize) attractive multiples of the sum that the customer has on deposit?

For example, the first prize multiple might be, say, three times the amount in the customer's account; the second prize twice the amount — and so on down to the smallest prize which might be half the customer's deposit.

Even though marketers tend to imitate each other slavishly, offering prize lists that consist entirely of cars, holidays, videos, TVs and computers — merchandise of one form or another — it might be a lot more effective to offer an incentive that is directly related and appropriate to the promoter's objective.

A prize structure on the lines described above is easily adaptable to other kinds of marketing objectives and has possibilities for many kinds of business.

A credit card company, for example, might both attract new customers and stimulate use of the card by those who already have one by promoting a contest — open exclusively to holders of the card — in which the prizes are multiples of the value of the winning customer's transactions in a given period — or multiples of the balance outstanding on the winners' accounts. So long as the winning customers show sufficient skill and judgement, the chance to win prizes can be made entirely conditional on spending money with the promoter of the contest. It would even be legal to offer as a prize a refund of all, or part, of the price of a purchase -whether of a car, a holiday or goods purchased at a retail outlet.

But none of the forms of prize that I have suggested would be legal if the chosen incentive was a sweepstakes, where entry cannot be confined to customers or those who spend or invest money with the promoter.

It is surprising how few direct marketers make use of the incentive potential of a contest, which — although admittedly more time-consuming and difficult to enter than a prize draw — provides much greater direct and explicit leverage in the process of moving people in the desired direction.

There is, however, one set of circumstances in which entry to a sweepstakes can legitimately be made conditional on acceptance of an offer. This is when the response that you seek takes the form of a request or order for something that the responder does not have to pay for. This might for example be a personal quotation for an insurance policy, or it might be an application for a store or credit card which is supplied free of charge to the holder.

What makes it legal to restrict sweepstakes entry to positive responders is the fact that the request or application involves neither payment nor obligation to make one (what lawyers refer to as "contribution" or "consideration"). The individual who seeks sweepstakes entry by responding positively remains perfectly free to decide not to accept the insurance quotation, and is under no obligation whatever to use the card — for which, remember, he has not had to pay.

It has to be recognised that the laws relating to lotteries and contests run for commercial purposes are enforced with less than total rigour. Moreover, enforcement itself is something of a lottery. Plenty of organisations seem to get away scot-free with running prize schemes that are technically illegal. An example is the type of scheme that offers prizes for the first x correct replies (to some simple question) "received", or "opened" by the promoter. Such schemes, although they may involve a small degree of skill, depend primarily on the element of chance.

Almost every day provides countless examples of this type of scheme — and also of others which are incontrovertibly illegal lotteries in which entrants must pay to take part. For those prepared to run the risk of prosecution, the commercial rewards can be substantial and the penalties of successful prosecution relatively small. For high-profile organisations the main risk is that of unfavourable publicity — the stigma of a conviction for a technical breach of the law. One suspects however that the public appetite for gambling of all kinds is now so voracious that few people would think any worse of an organisation convicted for a technical breach of arcane laws that command little understanding or respect.

Prompt-Reply Incentives

One proven prompt reply incentive is to offer a number — 50, 100 or more — worthwhile but not too costly prizes to the first 50, 100 or more (depending how many you can afford) replies that are "drawn". Note those two key words, *replies* (not "orders") and *drawn* (not "received"); either of these would in several jurisdictions make a perfectly legal scheme illegal — either as a draw that participants had, in effect, to pay to enter (by ordering the product); or as an illegal form of contest in which winning demands no skill at all, but simply speed in replying. But if you hold a draw open to all responders *after* replies have been received, you should be legally secure. It would however be legal to offer only orderers the chance to win a prize if you made the scheme a contest, with entry limited to those who ordered before a given deadline. In that case you would have to send an entry form to all who fulfilled the condition, and make sure that prizes were given only to the 100 or so best entries.

Lotteries and contests can be a legal minefield. But for those who tread with the confidence that knowledge gives, both these incentives can improve results dramatically.

You might incidentally be heartened to reflect that, even though — in the case of a draw — your copy reads *replies* and *drawn*, most people will in their own minds replace these with the two forbidden words "orders" and "received" rewarding you with extra orders sent more promptly. In the area of incentive copy, what you actually write is sometimes less important than what readers may choose to believe!

Sweepstakes Entry Forms

Crucial to the effectiveness of sweepstakes as an incentive is the *credibility* of the presentation. This is partly a matter of design but even more critically down to the copywriter's skill in convincing prospects that they have real chances to win. In some parts of the world sweepstakes have been given a bad name by companies which have come to depend on exaggeration as the only effective way of persuading their prospects to enter.

Although all that anyone need do to enter a sweepstakes is send in a piece of paper bearing a name and address, the majority of sweepstakes operators have found that it helps to design the entry document to give it an appearance of value and importance. As a result, there has grown up a practice of dressing up the entry form, so as to ape the appearance of documents that people recognise as of genuine importance — for example, legal or financial documents. Among users of sweepstakes there has developed a veritable industry devoted to producing what are really counterfeits — forms that mimic various official documents such as contracts, bank notes, licences and forms of computer stationery. The appearance of authority, seriousness and value that these documents have in common reflect the discovery by mailers that garish entry forms have on the whole been notably less successful than those which look "sincere" and serious.

But the frantic effort to find new and different ways to dress up the sweepstakes entry form absorbs substantial amounts of money, time and effort — an investment that is usually justified with the incantation "change of pace". There is in the business a widespread belief that people will only be interested in chances to win money if the opportunity to do so is continually presented to them in a different guise. It is rather as if an individual, lacking confidence, has managed to convince himself that he will only be of interest to those whom he encounters frequently if he keeps turning up in a different disguise — wearing, in succession, a fez, a turban, a solar toupee, a false moustache, a monocle — and so on through a repertoire of different props.

This tenacious faith in the value of "change of pace", while certainly correct in recognising the irritation felt by many at being bombarded with repetitious and boring sweepstakes mailings, seems to me to be missing the point about the remedy. After all, both the national lottery and football pool promoters succeed in appealing to millions of punters, and manage, week after week, to rake in prodigious sums of money by providing entry forms whose appearance never alters . . . indeed whose very familiarity is in fact one of their strengths. One is driven to speculate how many sweepstakes mailers have even tested the effect of mailing a standard, unvarying format to a group of customers, applying the "change of pace" concept to other components of the mailing package. Consistency and familiarity might do wonders for the credibility of sweepstakes mailings.

If sweepstakes mailers really believe in the value of changing the window dressing frequently, why do so few of them seem to do any radical testing, not just of the design of entry forms, but of the whole rationale and presentation of the sweepstakes offer.

Not long ago, when the headlines in Britain were dominated by stories about "sleaze", one or two members of parliament were accused of taking bribes in return for asking questions in the House on behalf of influential people who had a financial interest in the issue being raised. "Cash For Questions" became the slogan attached to this scandal, which the media reported obsessively and with relish. The phrase became so universally familiar that I wonder whether it might not provide the basis for a different and accurate presentation of the nature of a sweepstakes — which is, in essence, to offer "cash for *answers*":

> As a pleasant change from all the fuss about "Cash For Questions", here is a chance for you to take part in a draw that offers "CASH FOR ANSWERS". This letter brings you a chance to win a share, worth up to £100,000, in a total pay out of £250,000 cash for answers.
>
> Your one-word answer to a single, simple question could win you a cheque for up to £100,000, <u>tax-free</u>.

> Here's the question: "Would you like to see, on seven days' approval, without obligation to buy, our latest . . .?"

> The brochure that you will find enclosed with this letter gives all the reasons why it will pay you to say "Yes!"

Another credible, "change of pace" presentation of sweepstakes prizes might be "Response Rewards":

> £100,000 would be a pretty substantial reward just for answering this letter. Yet that — responding to this letter — is all you are asked to do for your chance to win one of 200 Response Rewards, ranging in value from £100 to £100,000. What is more, a prompt response could add a £5,000 bonus to the value of any reward that your response could win.

> Responding promptly to our offer could win you a valuable prize. £200,000 in Response Rewards is waiting to be won!

Sweepstakes Copy Themes

If you study the copy used by successful sweepstakes and contest mailers, several recurrent themes can be identified. One is *selection* — an assurance that chances to take part in a sweepstakes or a contest are not offered indiscriminately and that those who are lucky enough to be chosen can regard themselves as singularly favoured.

> Only a minority of Jackson residents will be lucky enough to receive chances to win in this sweepstakes. But I am glad to be able to tell you that when the names of the winners are announced one of them could turn out to live at 14 Fir Tree Road, and that the name on the first prize cheque for £50,000 could be Mrs R J Smith.

Progress

To make the possibility of winning more real and immediate — less distant and remote — some mailers have found that it helps to give readers the impression that they have already taken significant steps along the road to riches.

> **The draw for prizes worth £50,000 has already taken place, and you could be holding right now one of the sixty winning numbers. We know of course which these numbers are, but we don't yet know who holds them. So be sure to put in your claim by sending your numbers back for checking.**

Or again:

> **First with selection to receive a chance to win, and then with receipt of your official entry ticket, you've already taken two crucial steps along the road to winning. All that now remains is for you to post your ticket for entry in the draw for prizes worth £50,000.**

Recognition

People like to be recognised as customers, and made to feel that you value their business.

> **As someone with whom we've been doing business since 1986, you are one of the first to receive an invitation to enter this contest, in which £60,000 worth of prizes are waiting to be won by Wilson's customers.**

For reasons already explained, this kind of approach is more suitable for a contest than for sweepstakes.

Favouritism

Most of us enjoy being made to feel that we have been singled out for special favour.

**As a gold card holder you can look forward to receiving —
if your contest entry wins first prize — an invitation to
come to London to receive it. What is more, if the first
prize winner proves to be a gold card holder, we will add
to the £50,000 prize a special £10,000 bonus.**

Bonuses

Whether your draw is to take place before or after the mailing,
it is often valuable to build in an extra incentive to reply without
delay. This can for example be a bonus — a worthwhile sum of
money to be added to the biggest prize if the winner entered
swiftly. Or it can, in the case of a post-draw, be some special
extra prize for which only those who enter promptly will be eli-
gible.

The Downside of Sweepstakes

Despite what has been said so far concerning the value of
sweepstakes in direct marketing promotion, when it comes to
using this incentive I have to confess to being a sceptic, if not a
heretic. This is not because I doubt the value of sweepstakes in
boosting both response and orders. My scepticism centres on
the way the incentive is presented — and in particular on the
balance struck between the presentation of sweepstakes and
product.

A typical mailing piece will be totally dominated by the
sweepstakes. Recipients could be forgiven for concluding that
the mailer's reason for writing is to offer them chances to win.
The actual product or service being sold is almost eclipsed by
the graphics and copy devoted to the sweepstakes, and is relegated to what must often look more like a supporting than a
leading role.

One has to question whether this is really all that clever. I
don't doubt that, in the short term, it is effective in boosting
response. But I suspect that in the longer term allowing
sweepstakes to dominate the mailing package can be harmful.

There are at least five reasons why this should be so. In the first place, it conveys to many people an unsettling impression of dishonesty. They know perfectly well that you mailed them in the hope of selling something, not as a philanthropic exercise in giving them a chance to enrich themselves at your expense. There is thus a disturbing dissonance between the real and apparent reasons why you mailed them, which must arouse in some readers the suspicion that they are being conned.

Another effect of sweepstakes dominance is to down-grade in readers' eyes the importance and value of the product. If your mailing says less about the product than about the sweepstakes, the impression given is likely to be that there is not a lot to be said for it!

A third reason for doubting the wisdom of the conventional treatment of sweepstakes is that it may damage performance. Sweepstakes are undoubtedly effective in generating response, and consequently orders. But when somebody has placed an order primarily in the hope of winning a prize, the euphoria induced by the initial sweepstakes mailing may well not survive delivery of the product and the bill. The penalty could therefore be high rejections and poor payments.

There are two further significant reasons why domination of mailings by the sweepstakes element is a questionable strategy: the first is that it irritates the more intelligent consumers, who regard it as one of the characteristic indicators of "junk mail". Their hostility is echoed by consumer champions — self-appointed or official — and also by the proliferating regulatory organisations. This is one reason why I believe that the days of this practice may be numbered. It is becoming less and less respectable.

Conversely, the traditional package with sweepstakes saturation is most effective with the least intelligent; by definition, its strongest appeal is to the credulous. If what you want is to build up a mailing list made up in the main of the intellectually challenged, making intensive use of the traditional sweepstakes, "junk mail" package is probably the best way to go about it. If however you aspire to the creation of a list that you can keep approaching with offers of quality products, you might be well advised to give them a more prominent part in your mailing package.

Sweepstakes is, after all, an *adjunct* — an additional incentive to reply. Intelligently used, it will hold its value. But promotion above its true status to total dominance of the mailing package in my view not only erodes the credibility of the whole promotion; it also greatly increases the resemblance of one package to another, making it more difficult to distinguish one mailing — and one mailer — from another. This is particularly dangerous in cases where product and promotion flows are of high intensity, with packages thudding regularly onto the doormats of the people who make up the best lists. When, every time, the sweepstakes swamps the package, it must seem to the customer rather as if a pair of proud new parents were photographed holding the after-birth rather than the baby!

The archetypal sweepstakes package is familiar enough: a portentous-looking document that resembles nothing so much as a share certificate in a defunct South American mining company, replete with all the cartouches, scrolls and watermarks that one finds on obsolete bank notes.

The document's phraseology is equally pretentious, reading most often like a parody of some legal document, with a "Be it known . . ." here, a "Whereas . . ." there, and a "Hereinafter . . ." somewhere else. The belief is clearly that the credulous boobies who receive this pretentious package will be conned into believing that the sweepstakes promoter is contractually bound to pay them a pot of money. Indeed, in many cases the clear intention of the copywriter has been to convince the reader that he has miraculously won a prize already in a draw that he has not yet even entered.

Tacky, contrived and unconvincing, the whole thing has come to look like an exhibit in a museum of direct mail in its least scrupulous days.

And the copy in the accompanying letter? In about 1,500 overheated, ungrammatical words, this breathlessly informs (or, more likely, "advises") the reader that:

> In the event you win our fabulous first prize, you would be able to pay into your local Lake Woebegone Bank, or any other that you name, the sum of $1,000,000, that is ONE MILLION DOLLARS — to spend in any way you choose.

The copy then goes on to list for the benefit of less imaginative readers the implications of having such a well-nourished bank account, including the ability to "write checks for $50,000 . . . $20,000 and still have more than $500,000 to invest or spend"; not to mention the possibility of buying "that car you've always wanted" or "jetting off with a partner on the holiday of your dreams".

Sweepstakes packages like this drop daily through the letterboxes of households all over the world as sweepstakes mailers slavishly imitate each other, following the well-trodden sweepstakes path with the same blind faith displayed by the rats of Hamelin as they pursued the Pied Piper.

Easy enough to mock, you may be thinking, but what would you do instead?

What I would do is put the sweepstakes in its place — which is that of a powerful and valuable supporting element. Put the sweepstakes components inside a second, inner envelope, with the product components given pole position as the first thing the reader sees when he opens the outer envelope. This gives the incentive *prominence* (which it merits) without *dominance* — which in my view it should not have.

In short, my inclination is to treat the sweepstakes as I would a particularly attractive premium — making it impossible to overlook, without allowing it to overshadow the product. And I would encourage writers to talk about it, not in feverish, near-hysterical tones that lack all credibility, but in the level, civil, enthusiastic tone of voice of one who has something good to offer.

What some sweepstakes mailers seem to me to be doing is breeding a race of laboratory consumers with some very strange characteristics that combine increasingly to set them apart from the remainder of the human race. Junkmail Man (as I think of him) has, through a process of what might be termed 'Natural Deselection", become singularly adept at performing a number of pointless tasks that few people who have anything approximating to a life are any longer prepared to carry out.

Their characteristics — Darwinian adaptations that have won them their niche on the market — include the patience to wade through mountains of misleading and unconvincing verbiage, a readiness to humour those who mail them packages so packed with involvement and action devices that the best part of an hour can be happily spent ticking boxes, transferring adhesive seals and labels from one part of the package to another, rubbing away the plasticized surface of a panel to reveal a hidden message, inserting plastic tokens in little pouches and generally engaged in countless other patently absurd activities.

At a time when the media offer so many stimuli that compete for the public's attention, Junkmail Man must constitute a dwindling, ageing proportion of the market, whose characteristics of gullibility, stupidity and greed continue to exert a disproportionate influence on mailers who use sweepstakes, and on the image of the direct marketing business as a whole.

Premiums (Free Gifts)

Giving prominence to the premium is one of the keys to success. And one way to do this in a letter without disrupting the flow of what you want to write about the product is to feature it on an illustrated flap attached to page 3 of a four-page letter. Alternatively, a panel can be placed beneath the signature.

If you offer a free gift, try to describe it with relish and enthusiasm. If the writer doesn't sound enthusiastic, the reader is unlikely to find the gift desirable. ("Enthusiastic" does not mean bombastic or hysterical). A premium needs to be described in terms that, while remaining wholly credible, make

the reader feel that he will be getting something worthwhile —
useful, unusual, desirable. Often a free gift is presented in a
way that seems perfunctory, listless and routine.

Here are four different premiums described in a way that
does at least make the reader feel that he is getting something
worth having:

ONE MORE GOOD REASON FOR SUBSCRIBING
We will make you the present of this
Mont Blanc Classic pen.

There are some possessions — a handful only of élite arte-
facts, with world-famous names and instantly recognisable
distinction — that add a small frisson of pleasure to even
the most commonplace everyday action. Unquestionably
numbered among them is a Mont Blanc pen.

Each one is a joy to use — even if for no more demanding a
purpose than to sign a directive or scrawl your initials on a
memo.

Uncap the sleek and lustrous black barrel to reveal a pur-
poseful, torpedo-shaped gold plated nib — precision-
engineered to glide firmly, fluently across the page. Relish
the well-judged weight and perfect balance of the pen —
the manner in which it responds compliantly to the light-
est grip.

No make of pen has a better claim to being, if not mightier
than the sword, one of the most often-handled, benevo-
lent instruments of power. The signing of an important
document — be it a treaty or a contract — calls, by common
consent, for a pen of appropriate stature . . . a writing in-
strument that brings to the occasion a somewhat greater
dignity and presence than a well-chewed ball point or bat-
tered fibre tip! Such a sense of occasion so often prompts
the choice of a Mont Blanc — a pen whose familiar summit
emblem can be seen at many a political and commercial
summit meeting.

> Supplied in a slim and elegant case with a plush base and silk-lined lid, the Mont Blanc Classic is a pen made for the pockets of power. We are giving one free with each new subscription.

Or:

> Let me tell you about the present that we would like to send you with (product).
>
> It is, in fact, a clock — but no ordinary, run-of-the-mill clock. The one that we have chosen for you is a replica of an elegant timepiece that is famous all over the world as the product of a distinguished firm of jewellers. Only a few decades ago, a charming little clock like this would probably have cost a small fortune. Now, thanks to modern technology, the accuracy of a battery-powered quartz movement is available in a clock of gracious, traditional design. The case is of gleaming, polished brass, while black hour and minute hands — with gold second and alarm hands — make this a clock of unmistakable distinction, compatible with any decor, and light and compact enough to take with you on your travels.
>
> Made to the most exacting standards, this desirable little clock is in only limited supply. But we were able to secure enough to enable us to send you one as a present with (product) so long as your order reaches us within the next ten days.

Sometimes the copywriter is asked to describe a free gift that is not something calculated to set the pulses racing. But even one as unexciting as a bookplate can be made to sound worthwhile.

> Books are among the most desirable objects. But their size, and easy portability, has always made their owners vulnerable to less scrupulous friends! Books can be too easily borrowed, begged — or even stolen — by others who covet

them for the value and fascination of their contents, or for
the beauty of their illustrations and binding.

To safeguard their property, and identify the rightful
owner, lovers of good books have, by long-hallowed tradi-
tion, pasted inside the front cover a personal bookplate
that says to whose library the book belongs. To welcome
you to the Club, here are four personal "Ex Libris" book-
plates for you to paste inside the first four books that you
order from the Club. When you pay so little for books that
are worth so much you won't want to risk your bargains
going astray!

Or:

By way of a welcome to the ranks of our subscribers, we
would like to mark the occasion by making you a present
of this steel paper knife. Elegantly made in stainless steel
fashioned in the shape of a sword, this is a paper knife to
grace even the most opulent desk — a useful and elegant
reminder of one of the best decisions that you have ever
taken.

Often you see gifts presented in a routine, half-hearted way —
with a headline that drones FREE GIFT FOR YOU or YOURS AS A
FREE GIFT, followed by a perfunctory description and unap-
pealing illustration of the gift that is on offer. Usually, too, the
copy goes on to rub the reader's nose in the prompt order condition — makes him feel that the writer is ramming a gun in his
ribs: "But you <u>must</u> order within 10 days", or "<u>Provided</u> that you
order promptly".

Good copy does not hold the reader up to ransom — and
makes sure that while the prompt order condition is unmistakable, the reader is not made to feel that he is having his arm
twisted. Here is one way to do it:

With your (video, rose bush, membership card or whatever) you can look forward to receiving (whatever is of-

> fered as a premium — diary, alarm clock or whatever) as a
> thank you for your order. But stocks of this attractive clock
> are in limited supply. We can however guarantee that one
> of them is yours so long as your order reaches us within
> the next 10 days.

Copy like this does three things: it gives a reason for the deadline (limited supply); it makes the gift seem more like a grace-
ful gesture than a bribe. And it makes the prompt order condition plain (even the biggest idiot can work out that if the gift ac-
companies the product, the only way to receive it is to place an
order).

If you have a decent gift to offer make sure that you don't
under-sell it — describe it in the same enthusiastic terms as the
product that you are trying to sell. If it is not attractive, desirable or useful ask yourself whether it is worth having at all. If
the recipients are disappointed, they are likely to punish you
with poor payments and high rejections of the product.

Mystery Gifts

If the only premium that you can afford is such a dog that you'd
rather not have to describe it, you might like to consider the
possibility of featuring it as a "Mystery Gift". A mystery gift has
three things going for it. One is *greed* — the offer of something
for nothing will always have appeal; the second is *curiosity* —
people will want to find out what it is; the astonishing durability
of mystery gifts as a useful direct marking incentive represents
a triumph of hope over experience. No matter how many times
they have sent for a mystery gift, only to receive some distinctly
underwhelming object, people still live in hopes of one day receiving a lovely surprise.

The third advantage of a mystery gift as an incentive is that
since it is a mystery you can (if it is something that all who respond to your mailing will receive), send something better to
those who order the product than to those who don't. It is never
wise to disappoint your customers, so if you don't want them to

punish you with rejections and bad debts it would be wise to make sure that their mystery gift is something decent.

Which leads me to another observation. Suppose that you have managed to track down a premium which it would take only a small increase in pull to make cost effective, it might be even more effective as a mystery gift than as a gift that you describe. This is because what you want to do is to maximise response: the more replies to your offer that you receive (whether orders or refusals) the more orders you will get. This is why it can be smart to offer a mystery gift just for a reply.

Prohibitively costly? — Far from it. All you need do is ask those whose response is not an order to supply an envelope and postage for their mystery gift — which can of course be something inexpensive. Orderers on the other hand will receive with the product something which they should be pleased to get — something in fact which you might otherwise have been delighted to offer, and describe, as a free gift.

I make this suggestion simply to illustrate the point that there are many different ways of using premiums (a mystery gift being simply a premium that you have chosen not to describe).

"Gambles"

There is of course also more than one way to feature mystery gifts. One is simply to make it conditional on either order or response. Another would be to make the reader feel that he has "won" it by giving him some little game to play — giving the offer the appearance of a gamble. You might for example include in your mailing package a scratch-off card that replicates the familiar symbols of a fruit machine or pack of playing cards. The reader would be told that eligibility for a mystery gift would depend on finding, say, three matching symbols or a particular "hand" of playing cards. (Naturally, everyone is "lucky".)

People value more highly a reward which they think that they have earned, and more highly still a reward that looks as if it has been bestowed on them by fate. Many of us live in hopes of winning — whether on the pools, the horses or a lottery — hopes that for the vast majority are destined never to be realised. Although not quite in the same league as a win with Camelot or Ernie, the illusion of "winning" that such little games provide offers similar gratification to a successful gamble, with the added advantage of being free of cost or risk.

A long time ago, before creative ingenuity was constrained by codes of practice and ethical scruples (in fact, at a time when many copywriters had all the ethical sensitivity of estate agents and snake-oil salesmen) I became involved in a fascinating exercise.

A direct marketer wanted to test the value as a premium (for buying a gardening product) of a set of flower prints. We ran a three-way test: first, of a straightforward product offer without a premium; second of offering the prints as a free gift for buying the product. The third test presented the prints as a "prize" that the reader had "won" in a contest open to anyone responding to the offer.

The results were an eye-opener. The test of the prints as a free gift with the product pulled less than the no-premium control (i.e. actually reduced the pull); but when described as a "prize" that the reader had "won", the pull climbed significantly. There is a lesson here for every copywriter.

Earlier, I pointed out that the impulse to buy is quickly dissipated. It may not survive overnight or over a weekend. If it has been generated by a press or TV ad you have therefore lost a sale.

The direct marketer is in a stronger position. He can provide prospects with an opportunity to take decisive action instantly by including in a direct mail package some sort of action device — something the reader can use on the spot to signify acceptance of the offer. Whatever form it takes — a seal or a stamp to stick, a box to tick, or a metal or plastic token to return — the use of this action device gives people something to do which serves to signal acceptance of the offer. It fulfils much the same function as the ring in a marriage ceremony.

Discounts and Savings

In the course of every sales pitch there comes a moment when you have to reveal what acceptance of your offer would cost. Since this may well prove an unpalatable pill for the customer to swallow, it is smart to sugar it in one of the many ways available to the skilful copywriter. If you are able to offer a discount, it will certainly pay to do so. And if you can plausibly do so it is politic to justify the discount in some way . . . "As an introduction to . . ." or as "A special privilege for our account customers".

Discounts can arouse suspicion. A famous advertising anecdote concerns the New York department store that ran a stock disposal promotion for television sets. Drastic price reductions failed to shift the stock, and the management discovered that customers suspected the sets would not be offered at such low prices unless they were in some way defective.

Then someone came up with a bright idea to justify the price reduction: he went round with a pin and slightly scratched each set, putting up placards that proclaimed "Huge reductions on slightly damaged stock!" The shelves were cleared in hours. It usually helps to *justify* the bargain.

But even if you can't offer a discount, there must still be something you can do to make the price *seem* small — for example, by comparing it with prices of similar products, or the cost of getting the same service or benefit in another way.

> **The price you are paying for our book is less than a quarter of a solicitor's (or doctor's or accountant's) fee for a half-hour consultation on a single problem; for this amount you get X00 pages of expert, professional advice on a vast range of legal (or medical or financial) problems." Judiciously chosen comparisons can make the price seem small, the product appear better value.**

There can be no escaping the fact that any purchase is "for real". That's why it is smart to offer readers hard-nosed practical justifications for spending money on your product, even if their real motivation is some private dream.

Chapter 8

Business-to-Business Selling

It is a mistake to imagine that it is necessary to adopt some special tone of voice simply because readers are being approached in their capacity as business people. They do not abandon on coming to work the whole range of human aspirations, prejudices, preferences, anxieties and ambitions which motivate them in their home environment.

It never ceases to surprise me how many mailers who are trying to promote a product or service to business users attempt to do so in what they clearly imagine to be a tone of voice that is "appropriate". This usually takes the form of the kind of turgid, pretentious "executive-speak" in which so many appointments vacant ads are couched, as if Business Man and his female colleagues were a different species, able to communicate only in pompous polysyllables.

What is essential when approaching people in their business role is to bear in mind that, on top of the characteristics that they have in common with everybody else, there will be a significant business dimension to any decision that they make about your offer. Obviously, you need to make it easy for them to justify (if only to themselves) expenditure of the company's money. So naturally the benefits you offer, the promises you make, the empowerment that you claim for your product, need to be set firmly in a business context . . . the advantages of purchase need to be, not only personal, but corporate.

This is one reason why offers of free gifts need to be handled with caution, and sensitively phrased. Some managers would be likely to feel guilty about accepting anything that might be perceived as being in the nature of a bribe or reward for spending the company's money. So it might be better to choose as an incentive something with a corporate as well as a personal dimension (such as, for example, a desk diary or a dictaphone).

One barrier that you will have to surmount is the zealous secretary or personal assistant, determined to act as a filter for her boss and to keep out of the in-tray anything that seems irrelevant or trivial. It can therefore be useful sometimes to mail more than one of the firm's executives, and to enable each of them to see that others (including perhaps the MD or CEO) are being copied with the letter — and might therefore be interested in the principal addressee's response.

Another stratagem (mentioned under "Hitting The Right Targets") is attachment to the letter of a circulation slip listing by function the managers who might be interested: "Finance Director, Chief Accountant, Credit Manager" and so on.

One consideration that may well be influential with business readers is the number of other employees of the business who might arguably benefit from acceptance of your offer. This is certainly the case where the product or service can credibly be described as *educational*, for example, a training course, book or subscription to a trade or business magazine.

Not only is there the possibility that acceptance of your offer might take the form of a multiple order. Managers often spend the company's money more freely when they are buying, not for themselves, but on behalf of other putative beneficiaries. They might for example conclude that a trade magazine, although of no interest whatever to them, could prove of immense benefit to the accountancy staff or the sales force. It is often an advantage when the decision to purchase, or renew, is taken by somebody other than the ostensible beneficiaries who — left to their own devices — might well refuse the offer.

Two more points to bear in mind: it is only tactful to ensure that your copy is seen to conform with the reader's likely self-image as a hard-pressed manager with no time to waste. And if an addressee can be identified by name as well as function you might reasonably mark the outer envelope as "Personal".

Here are some examples of business-to-business approaches, couched — not in the clotted prose of "executive-speak" — but in direct, business-like language.

Time was when a senior financial executive could make the company's fortune, and a personal reputation, simply by applying experience and judgement to what was read on the train in the pages of the *Wall Street Journal* or the *Financial Times.*

Now the pace of events is such, the techniques of financial management so sophisticated, that the successful financial executive depends on a constant flow of <u>information</u> — intelligently gathered, expertly interpreted, carefully selected and succinctly presented in a form that makes it easy for busy readers to absorb it quickly.

That's why in solving the range of financial problems that pass across your desk — from valuing a company to raising long-term debt, from managing risk to interpreting trends in different sectors of the market, from assessing the investment potential of a foreign country to analysing the implications for your company of new legislation — you will come to prize the support and assistance you are offered every month in the pages of — .

FINANCIAL INTELLIGENCE SERVICE

The quality, range and depth of the information, analysis and comment that this respected financial journal brings you every month are unrivalled. Together its hand-picked team of contributors and editors — enjoying, as they do, the confidence of key corporate and banking players — provide readers of the .... with a financial intelligence service of the highest calibre . . . greatly valued by them for its authority, integrity and impartiality.

Here for example, culled at random, are just a few of the insights that you would have gained from recent issues:

Or:

The distribution list at the head of this letter indicates the kind of reader for whom the authoritative international journal — is designed. Although most staff at senior levels will find its contents of interest, this influential monthly magazine will be of greatest interest and value to the higher echelons of management, where the crucial financial decisions are taken.

In taking those decisions one need is paramount: reliable, up-to-date information — intelligently gathered from all over the world and presented clearly and concisely.

Every month, in the pages of ....- you will find the news and views, the facts and figures that you need to take informed decisions . . . news from home and abroad, and from various sectors of the market . . . analysis techniques . . . information that is vital to the successful management of change, equipping you to react effectively and fast to fresh challenges and new problems.

Opportunities, ideas, analyses, forecasts, news, opinions . . . these are just some of the things that — will bring you month by month — crisply presented in a handsome format specifically designed to make it easy for busy readers to absorb its contents quickly.

Or:

With recession tightening its grip on the economies of many nations, now more than ever you need reliable intelligence in the military sense of <u>information</u>.

For financial executives, bankers and institutional inves-
tors — those who take everyday decisions that can make
or break companies and people — the most trusted and reliable source of financial intelligence is the respected international journal .... a monthly magazine that is read
throughout the world by senior officers of banks, insurers,
market makers, Government departments, financial regu-
lators and corporate finance departments.

Recent research among international financial managers
has shown that in the boardrooms and offices of the
world's top 3000 companies, the most widely read magazine is —, now considered essential business reading by
financial professionals responsible for underwriting, forex,
new issues, corporate finance, project finance, risk management and swaps.

Each monthly issue provides a balanced, authoritative
blend of in-depth analysis, accurate prediction, inside information and exclusive revelations which together throw
light on every corner of the world of international financial management.

Or:

HOW TO GET AN INCENTIVE SCHEME OR A
CONFERENCE OFF THE GROUND

In the course of your business you must often have occasion to take decisions concerning the movement of sizeable parties by air.

Overseas travel — especially to one of the more exotic destinations — provides a highly attractive and effective way
to motivate key people . . . employees, sales force, distribu-
tors, dealers and agents. While a conference held abroad
affords an opportunity to recharge business batteries in a
stimulating setting.

For both the purposes I have mentioned — incentives or conference travel — there are sound and substantial business reasons for bringing your problems to ....

Experience

We have more than 20 years' experience of this highly specialised market, and a solid record of success in arranging incentive and conference travel for organisations in Britain — including a number of famous companies.

Resources

We have a world-wide computerised reservations system that will book you a seat or a bed (or should you need one, a baby's bassinet!) at the touch of a button. And our Hotel System provides a network of 72 fine hotels around the world — at all of which the traveller can be certain of a welcome.

Value

Cost will of course be a major factor in your choice, and if you think of — as expensive the prices we can quote you could come as an agreeable surprise. Substantial group discounts are available on parties of 7 or more people on both fares and hotel charges. Moreover, the cost to companies of business conferences are normally tax-deductible. As one of the principal agencies for bringing Western travellers to Asia, we are better placed than most to secure favourable rates at our country's leading hotels. We can also quote highly competitive prices for your travel to Rome, Delhi and Bangkok."

Or:

HOW TO KEEP YOUR ADVERTISING
OUT OF QUEER STREET

Queer Street (and, probably, Carey Street too) is a one-way street. The advertising traffic moves in one direction only: outwards from the advertisers.

On Easy Street, traffic moves in both directions. As well as the outgoing traffic there is a healthy flow of orders and enquiries in the opposite direction.

As more and more companies are finding, <u>direct response advertising pays</u>. It is economical, measurable and highly cost-effective. And to help you make the most of the opportunities provided by this uniquely effective medium, nobody is better equipped and qualified than ....

Or:

A SALESMAN'S FOOT IS NOT THE MOST EFFECTIVE WAY TO OPEN DOORS!

A boot thrust roughly into a fast-closing gap is one way to open the door to a selling message. But it is neither tactful nor effective.

A more agreeable and efficient way to open customers' doors to your products is the — self-mailer.

A unique, efficient and highly cost-effective salesman, the - — self-mailer (of which this is one example) is a self-contained piece that incorporates, <u>in just one document</u>, a striking and colourful cover, a powerful selling message and a compelling reply device.

Or:

YOUR LIST OF ASSETS COULD BE WORTH A LOT MORE THAN YOU THINK!

The list we have in mind consists of the names and addresses of your customers: one of the greatest assets of your business — and one that, almost certainly, is a great deal more valuable than you might imagine.

If you're not using .... self-mailers to approach your list — to generate orders, elicit enquiries or create fresh leads for salesmen — you're not getting the kind of return on your assets that your business needs if it is to expand and prosper.

Or:

SUBSTANTIAL SAVINGS ON YOUR OWN AND YOUR COMPANY'S TRAVEL BILL

Significant reductions in the prices of hotel accommodation . . . a swifter, smoother passage through check-in counters and departure lounges: these are just some of the benefits to which you could look forward as a regular reader of …………

That's not just a claim — it's a promise. A promise that we back with this unconditional guarantee: if after the first issue you are not convinced that — will save you many times the cost of your subscription (a business expense, by the way, that is fully tax-deductible) we will refund your subscription in full without question.

Among all the papers (passports, visas, permits and the like) that help to ensure our progress round the world, one is prized by the experienced traveller on business. Carried by seasoned travellers of many nationalities, it is the monthly magazine called —, whose contents . . . diverse and varied as they are . . . all have a common purpose: to ease, speed and cut the cost of business travel.

The fact that you're spending the company's money does not of course mean that you use it with any less care than you spend your own. And — could save your company a small fortune in air fares alone. Nor do the savings end with the purchase of your ticket. — tells you how the price of staying at a first class hotel can be cut by up to 40 per cent.

Or, finally,

The Consumer's Coin

Given the job of promoting the superior potential of some journal or TV station as a medium for high-pulling direct-response advertising, most copywriters would reach wearily for the usual socio-economic demographic statistics (proportion of viewers in the ABC 1 groups, proportion who own more than one car, etc); the in-trays of marketing and advertising managers are crammed with this kind of promotion.

More striking and likelier to secure attention might be a mailing piece that promised to explain how the reader could win "the most prestigious of all advertising awards — the "Consumer's Coin". The copy might then poke gentle fun at the profusion of statuettes and putty medals that the advertising industry likes to dish out to its members in order to dramatise the highly relevant claim that, at the end of the day, the only award that is really worth winning is the money spent by consumers in response to effective advertising. The mailing piece would include a nicely-packaged coin nestling in a cardboard reproduction of the velvet-lined case in which it is customary to house a medal.

Everybody in advertising is of course well aware that winning the patronage of consumers is what the industry is all about. But a mailing like this which reminds them that, when self-congratulation is over, the consumer's money is the most prestigious and coveted award of all should win favourable attention for a medium that can plausibly claim to be ideal for advertisers who seek a direct and measurable response.

Chapter 9

Handling Complaints and Getting Bills Paid

How to Apologise and Handle Complaints

When something has gone wrong it is usually better to level with the customer and admit fault frankly before a complaint has been made. You would be ill-advised to try to make light of the mistake. If you have let a customer down or caused him disappointment, what he wants to know is *why*; he would also like to know what you propose to do about it, and when he can look forward to receiving satisfaction. Customers are likely to feel bad about your failure and may be reassured to know that you feel bad about it too. What is more, when a cock-up has occurred they will want to be assured that you are doing everything possible to get your act together.

It is better for an apology to be volunteered, rather than wait to have it wrung from you reluctantly.

> We owe you an apology. I am afraid that, by the time your order reached us, stocks of our Chamois wristwatch were temporarily exhausted. Naturally, when our catalogue was mailed, we thought we had ample supplies. But I have to confess that on this occasion we simply got our sums wrong.

> Fresh supplies have been ordered from the manufacturer and should reach us in early July. I will of course make sure that you are sent one of the first to arrive. Meanwhile, I

should like to thank you for your order and apologise
again for having to keep you waiting for your watch.

Or:

Thank you for the completed proposal form that you sent
us recently. The scale of response to our insurance offer
has exceeded even our expectations. I'm afraid therefore
that stocks of the briefcase that we are giving away free to
new policyholders are temporarily exhausted.

A fresh supply will reach us shortly. But rather than keep
you waiting for your policy document, we are sending this
to you now. Your gift of a briefcase will be despatched under separate cover just as soon as we have further stocks —
which should be in early July.

Letters of Complaint

Any business that deals direct with customers is certain to
generate correspondence. Some of this will take the form of
protest and complaints. Replying to complaints from customers and members of the public is a more important function
than many seem to think. Skilfully handled, a mollified complainant can in the long run prove to be a more loyal and better customer than many who have never had occasion to complain. What is more, you never know if the complainant could
be somebody of influence whose opinion of your services and
products might influence the views of others. It is therefore
worth taking the trouble to ensure that complaints receive a
prompt, appropriate and well-calculated response.

There are in my experience one or two guidelines which
can help you to frame the right kind of response.

Be Polite

No matter how unreasonable a complaint, or how intemperately
it is phrased, it is never good practice to send a curt, dismissive
or contemptuous reply. Notwithstanding the old commercial

cliché, the customer is *not* always right, so it is not necessary always to agree with him or accept every complaint. There is however an important distinction between rejecting or refuting a complaint, and a civil explanation of your grounds for non-acceptance.

> Thank you for your letter of July 15. I am sorry that you should have taken exception to the fact that the investments listed in our recent offer happened to include pork belly futures.
>
> I can readily understand that, as a lifelong vegetarian and supporter of animal rights, you might find such a product distasteful. Nevertheless, the fact is that this commodity is proving popular with investors and we feel that we have an obligation to offer customers as wide a choice as possible of sound investments — subject always, of course, to current legal and ethical requirements.
>
> You will I am sure have noticed that the list of investments you received featured many that could arouse no ethical qualms of any kind, and I hope that among them you may find some that cause you no misgivings.

Or:

> Thank you for your letter of April 5. My colleagues and I read your comments with interest, and you can rest assured that they will be carefully considered. Meanwhile I should like to thank you for taking the trouble to write.

Or:

> Thank you for your letter of April 4. I was extremely concerned to learn that, in spite of the care with which all our products are packaged, the decanter that you ordered proved on delivery to have suffered slight damage in transit.

This is therefore to confirm that a replacement has already
been despatched, which should reach you within the next
few days. Meanwhile I would ask you to be kind enough
to return the damaged article in the carton in which it arrived, using the enclosed reply-paid label for the purpose.

Show That You Take It Seriously

Whether a complaint is justified or not, never give someone
the impression that it is being taken lightly. It might therefore
be wise to get your letter signed by somebody who sounds
reasonably senior. It doesn't need to be the Chairman or Managing Director; the Tufton-Buftons who — along with plenty of
perfectly reasonable people with fully justified complaints —
bulk large in a company's postbag don't always take kindly to
receiving replies to complaints which they addressed to the
Managing Director signed by a functionary with some such
title as "Correspondence Clerk", or "Customer Service Assistant". The aim should be to convey the impression that a
complaint has been taken seriously by somebody of consequence who has taken the time in a crowded day to write a
considered reply.

> I am sorry that you should have taken exception to (what-
> ever gave offence). Along with one or two senior col-
> leagues, I have read your comments with interest and you
> can rest assured that they will be carefully considered.
> Meanwhile I should like to thank you for taking the trou-
> ble to write.

Make Amends

If a complaint is justified you need to make amends. It is unwise
to do this grudgingly. When you are at fault it is better to admit
it frankly and make a generous gesture. A fatal mistake is to try
and dodge responsibility for a cock-up by attempting to retreat
behind a smoke-screen of waffle.

> I was extremely concerned to learn that one of our employees should have given you cause to complain. It is clear that your complaint is fully justified, and I should like to offer you a full and unreserved apology.

Or:

> Thank you for your letter. Clearly we owe you an apology. And as some compensation for the inconvenience you have suffered, we should like you to accept the gift of this (whatever). It comes with our sincere apologies for a mistake which I can promise you that we shall do our level best to prevent happening again.

On many occasions I have been saddled with the job of drafting replies to letters of protest or complaint that were addressed to a senior member of the Board. Drafting a letter that puts the Chairman's head above the parapet is an exercise that tends to concentrate the mind!

> Thank you for your letter of June 15 addressed to our Managing Director. Before leaving for a business trip abroad Mr Williams asked me to reply.

> I am glad to be able to reassure you that no irreplaceable natural resources have been lost at any stage of the process whereby the paper used to print our mailings is produced. The wood pulp is made from trees that have been grown for the purpose, and for every one felled a replacement is planted.

> Here at the Williams Corporation we share in full measure your concern for the environment and are determined to play our part in promoting forestry methods that are ecologically sound.

> Mr Williams has asked me to thank you for taking the trouble to write, and I hope that this reassurance will have set your mind at rest.

Or:

> Thank you for your letter of March 5 on the subject of sweepstakes prizes. I am of course sorry to hear that you have not yet been fortunate enough to win a prize. I can, however, assure you that there is no truth whatever in the assertion that not all the advertised prizes are actually awarded.
>
> Our records contain ample evidence that, of the xxx prizes offered since our sweepstakes started in 1993, every single one has been awarded to a winner. The total value of prizes advertised comes to £500,000 and our auditors can confirm that prizes of exactly this value have been accepted by winners.
>
> Thank you however for taking the trouble to write. We are always interested to learn customers' views on our sweepstakes. Provided that you keep on entering, I hope that in due course your perseverance may be rewarded with one of the valuable prizes.

Don't Argue

When replying to a complaint, try not to be argumentative. Tempting though it often can be to put someone who has asked for it in his place, it is wise to resist the temptation.

Getting Bills Paid

The lesson that "no sale has been made until the customer has paid" was one that I learned as soon as I entered the business. In those days, bills and collection letters used to be written by a copywriter skilled in the arts of coaxing money out of people's pockets. Today such documents tend to be the products of committees composed in the main of accountants, lawyers, computer technicians and credit managers. As a result, most of them are bland, featureless documents that have about as much impact on debtors as marshmallows hurled at the turret of an armoured car.

On the realistic scale of priorities that governs most people's attitude to paying bills, self-interest ranks much higher than any sense of obligation to creditors. While some pay promptly, the majority have an in-built preference for procrastination, and refuse to take bills seriously until the ink turns red.

So long as debtors believe they are getting standard treatment, they conclude quite correctly that plenty of others are still in the same boat. This is why stock letters and inflexible modules for billing so often fail to motivate debtors to pay. Once your billing series has creamed off prompt payers early in the series, you will be left with a substantial, thick-skinned rump of tardy payers and a sump into which — if allowed to do so — will drain potential delinquents.

The sooner, therefore, that debtors can be led to believe that their failure to pay is exceptional behaviour of a kind that places them in an exposed minority, the sooner they can be motivated to respond. Like school children they respond more readily to what they perceive as individual attention.

The paradox that bedevils every billing series is that, although the potential is obviously greatest early in the series when numbers are largest, little *pressure* to pay can be applied at such an early stage. So, although early billing efforts need to be effective, customers would be likely to take offence if you made them too aggressive.

An effective billing series needs therefore to be *orchestrated* — proceeding from the relatively laid-back tone of the early billing efforts, through more and more urgent requests for payment, to the penultimate and final demands. Pressure to pay should mount steadily through the series, with a substantial element of change of pace in the tone and appearance of the packages. An important creative objective should be to convey the impression that recipients are not just getting "bog standard" billing treatment, but personal, individual demands for payment.

Within the framework of these overall guidelines, there is plenty of scope for creative ingenuity — subject to the proviso that, generally speaking, a bill ought to look like a bill. What you choose to send with it can, however, take any form you choose.

One possibility — usable early in the series — is a bill that has an element of charm. One billing series that I recall being sent to buyers of a garden book made appropriate use of the "language of flowers" which happened to be one of the subjects covered by the book. A compliments slip bearing an illustration of a spring of rosemary carried this appropriately floral message:

> In flower language, memory
> Is symbolised by rosemary;
> We're sending you this sprig to say
> "Remember, please, to pay today!"

This slip was of course accompanied by a perfectly orthodox bill.

Once billing is seen as a promotion — rather than a legal or accountancy — function, a whole range of creative possibilities is opened up.

Velvet Glove

In many jurisdictions — both national and state — the question of what is permissible in billing efforts can be a legal minefield. In particular, there may be restrictions on the use of threats. It might however be possible to adopt the practice of some government departments and send a document that features various messages of a kind that the department might have occasion to send. Whichever of these is the operative message is indicated, either with a tick, or by crossing out all the messages that are in this instance inapplicable. The messages listed could span a wide spectrum of urgency and pressure. The obvious advantage of this approach is that it enables you to hint at the lengths to which the organisation is prepared to go to recover a debt, without actually threatening the recipient. (Of course, if a threat *is* intended, that is the message indicated with a tick.)

Humour

One attraction of using humour as a means of persuading customers to pay is that the suggestion alone is usually enough to wind up an accountant! Another good reason is that if several orthodox, conventional approaches in succession have failed to secure a payment, there has to be a good case for trying something different.

Urgency

The conventions of telegraphic language convey a sense of urgency — useful when payment is overdue but not to an extent which would justify a threat.

Quasi-legal Documents

Not every document that looks "legal" has to be issued by a Court or a lawyer. Instead of a summons or a writ you can, with the help of a good designer, create your own "payment is overdue" billing format — "Notice of Overdue Account" and the like.

Here is an example of a billing series which, as it progresses, applies escalating pressure to pay:

1st Bill
Prompt payment of the amount now due would be appreciated.

2nd Bill
The amount shown is now overdue. Please send payment immediately.

3rd Bill
Settlement of this account is now SERIOUSLY OVERDUE. Please send payment without further delay.

4th Bill

Despite repeated requests for payment, this bill remains unpaid. If payment is not received within 7 days the account will be passed for recovery to a debt collection agency.

As we have seen, a billing series should be orchestrated — with pressure to pay immediately being steadily increased throughout the series. However, this does not mean that each billing letter in the sequence should follow a conventional pattern. In fact, I believe that the use of unorthodox approaches may significantly boost the chance of securing the customer's attention, and consequently of getting him to pay.

Here are some less orthodox approaches to billing copy:

The Chief Accountant presents his compliments, and believes you would wish to be informed that the sum now due in respect of your recent purchase of (whatever) amounts to £37.50.

Copy such as this would be appropriate early in the series. If you are looking for something to send at a later stage, it might be smart to mail a tougher message modelled on the kind of letter sent by banks to customers who are slightly overdrawn:

At the close of business on (date) the amount overdue on your account was £37.50. Kindly send payment immediately, and refrain from sending further orders until the sum outstanding has been paid.

A hint of the possibility of a personal visit from a representative of the company to whom money is owed is likely to galvanise a debtor. This is why the inclusion with a letter from, say, the Chief Accountant or Credit Manager of a business card can work wonders later in the series.

Here is one more example of the use of humour in a billing series:

Our Credit Manager worries all the time. Right now he is worried sick about unpaid bills, and the click of his worry-beads is driving us all mad.

As an act of kindness, to him and the rest of us, please send payment <u>now</u>.

For many direct marketers who allow customers credit, an improvement in collection efforts represents the likeliest source of a swift and substantial boost to profits. Improved — and earlier — payments go straight onto the bottom line.

Chapter 10

Retention, Renewal
and Regeneration

It is sometimes said that customer loyalty is a thing of the past. And while it is certainly true that the days of fierce consumer loyalty to companies and brands have probably vanished for ever — that today people shop around for the best they can find in the way of value and service — there is still plenty that can be done to persuade customers to keep spending money with you. These can be summed up in a sentence — *treat them well*. This is more than a matter of consistently giving them good value and prompt, efficient service. It implies a consideration for their interests that can be demonstrated in a lot of different ways, many of them small, and most of them shown in the way that leading Internet companies like Amazon.com treat their customers. And they all involve a copywriter who provides the company with a message and tone of voice that are appropriate.

Acknowledge and Confirm an Order Swiftly

And (it should be added) express appreciation of it. To thank people for spending money with you is both common courtesy and sound business practice.

Say When Delivery Can Be Expected

Few things are more irritating than ordering a product and then being left hanging in the air wondering whether you order is being processed, and how long it will be before you receive it.

It used to be common, and is still not at all rare, to find in press ads, or somewhere in a mailing shot, a passage — usually in extremely small print — that says something like "Allow 28 days for delivery". The fact that customers were still prepared to order anything from companies which so clearly signal the fact that the interests of consumers are subordinated to their own time-honoured leisurely ways of doing business — in other words that they were driven by traditional and probably inefficient systems, rather than by a determination to give prompt, efficient service — can only be explained on the assumption that people never actually read these caveats.

People who locate on the Internet something that they want to buy naturally expect to get it quickly. By making it quick and easy for customers to find what they want, the Internet is speeding up the pace, as well the scale, of competition. To stay up with the leading players in the game — never mind ahead of them — you need to look at all possible ways of enhancing customer perception of the service you provide.

Make Them Feel Good About Doing Business with You

Don't just pack up and send off whatever the customer has ordered without including in the package something — a note or a letter — that helps to make the recipient feel good about purchasing from you. This need be nothing more elaborate than a message on these lines:

> *Here, with many thanks for your payment, is the widget that you ordered. With it you will find full instructions on its use and maintenance which will I hope help you to get the best out of this high-quality product.*

> **In the unlikely event that you have any problem with it, our Customer Helpline on (contact details) will be pleased to give you assistance and advice.**
>
> **It has been a pleasure to serve you on this occasion, and we look forward to another opportunity to do so.**

If the customer has been promised a gift, or a chance to win in a sweepstakes or contest, your enclosure should refer to this as well. The incentive will probably be well to the fore-front of the customer's mind, and failure to refer to it looks odd.

I once had dealings with a company whose up-front promotion made much of the "mystery gift" that was promised to those who bought the product. This gift arrived packed with the product, a book, that was itself encased for safety in yards of cardboard packaging. I forget now the nature of the gift, but it was something so small as to be all too easy to overlook, or even to distinguish from the packaging. Some passing reference to it in the letter would have helped to allay irritation and suspicion, as also would an assurance that I would, as promised, be entered in the sweepstakes and told if I was lucky enough to win a prize.

This kind of follow-through on the up-front promotion message helps to maintain incentive credibility, and is all part of making customers feel good.

Add Value

Apart from supplying what customers have specifically ordered, there are several ways in which e-marketers can enhance perception of the value they provide. A number of things can contribute to this concept of "added value". They include of course *information* — news of new and relevant services and products . . . news about developments such as changes to the law, or shifting market trends, that are likely to be of interest to a customer . . . facts about relevant research discoveries.

Providing customers with access to an information website that is constantly updated is one way to strengthen ties and en-

courage further contact. So, too, is the practice of sending customers further offers on privileged, or demonstrably favourable, terms.

A lot of these things can be done by e-mailing customers a
regular newsletter — possibly one that incorporates a "hotlink"
that provides them with an opportunity to click back for further
information.

Essentially the concept of added value boils down to one
very simple thing, which is by no means confined to doing
business on the Internet: the key to making people feel good,
and getting them to think about you in a positive way, is to do
whatever you can, not just to live up to their expectations of
you, but if possible go one better and exceed them. To get
something, however small, more than you expected of a vendor
is totally disarming. It engenders warm, positive feelings about
a supplier that can lead naturally and easily to further purchases.

Think of the last time you booked into a hotel and found in
your bedroom something a little better than you expected —
something a little more interesting than the traditional bowl of
unripe fruit, or a melting piece of chocolate on the pillow.
Even something as small and inexpensive as a cordial personal letter of welcome from the manager helps to make a new
arrival feel pleased that he booked in at this hotel. A few well-
chosen words is all it sometimes takes to encourage guests to
make another visit. And a few well-chosen words based on the
principles outlined in this book are all that it takes to distinguish good copy on the Internet from the truckloads of gar-
bage that daily jam the "information superhighway".

It is easier, and generally less expensive, to hang on to the
customers you have, rather than have to find new blood to replace the ones you lose. Hence the importance, not only of
continuing to supply them with good products; but also of
giving them good service and making them feel good.

So don't just bombard them with offers. Try to present each
offer that you make as being in the nature of a service — a re-

sponse to the customer's needs and interests, rather than a series of aggressive initiatives taken by the vendor.

This is where it helps to have on your database information volunteered by customers themselves about their needs and interests in response to market research or "Customer Surveys". People's willingness to divulge such information depends largely on how you present the request for such details. Try not to make it look like an attempt simply to discover ways to sell them more, and make more money from them. It is wiser to make your research seem more like a genuine effort on your part to provide an even better service.

Clearly from the nature of the purchases they've made it is possible to deduce much about your customers' interests and problems. These deductions can be used by copywriters to make subsequent offers seem like components of a service tailored to the interests of the customer.

> **Because of the interest you've shown in Italian cooking, you are naturally one of the first to be offered our new guide to Italian wines.**

In such ways a skilful copywriter can use a small amount of knowledge about a customer to help to build an impression of a continuing relationship that the vendor is keen to strengthen and develop. This impression is more easily created by giving the customer benefits and privileges such as premiums and discounts that can be credibly presented as a special reward for favoured customers.

These rewards are especially valuable if the relationship is cyclical and needs regular renewal — as is the case for example with some insurance policies, magazine subscriptions or "club" memberships. Don't be seen to be taking renewal for granted; offer the customer an incentive to continue — a reward for remaining on board.

Sometimes it is possible to detect impending defection and to take preventive action. If a customer has bought nothing for some time — despite having received many opportunities to do so — it is reasonable to deduce that he may be dissatisfied or bored. In such cases there is much to be said for some overt recognition of the fact that some time has elapsed since the customer's last purchase:

> It is, I see, more than two years since we last had the pleasure of receiving an order from you — in spite of the fact that in recent months we have made you several offers. Probably the fault is ours for not making you an offer more suited to your interests. However, I feel confident that you would not wish to miss the opportunity at least to see our latest (product). For I do not think that anyone with an interest in (whatever) could fail to be impressed by it.
>
> And because you have been such a good customer, we invite you, not only to see it on approval; if, as we believe, you are sufficiently impressed to wish to buy, we'll be happy to give you a special 10 per cent discount.

If, despite your best efforts to keep him, you lose a customer it is often possible to get him back into the fold with a message such as this:

> Nobody likes to lose touch with a friend — especially one like you who has long been a valued member.
>
> That's why I am sending you this personal invitation to rejoin on favourable terms which provide comprehensive insurance in return for easy quarterly payments. What is more, if you rejoin within 10 days, we will make you a present of a handsome fashion watch illustrated on the leaflet enclosed with this letter.

Or:

> I was concerned to learn that your membership has lapsed. Because you are not at the moment entitled to call on us for help I am sending you this personal invitation to rejoin.

> If you would like to regain the benefits of membership, we would be happy to welcome you back on the specially favourable terms to which a former member is entitled. Not only would the usual Enrolment Fee be waived; your membership would cost you only £x.

Or:

> We don't like to lose touch with any of our members, even when, as sometimes happens, they allow their membership to lapse.

> And if you would like to regain the benefits of membership, we would be happy to welcome you back on the especially favourable terms available to a former member; not only will we waive the usual enrolment fee; we will be happy to make you the present of a handsome watch.

A message like this can be adapted to suit the nature of many services and products. It can even be used to good effect by a charity. The essential components are an assurance that the reader has been missed as a customer, member or donor, coupled with the announcement of some special reason for coming back into the fold. This can be some new and particularly interesting product, a substantial improvement in service or price, or some good cause that provides the occasion for an especially important appeal.

Chapter 11

How to Raise Funds for Charities

Among the advice — some good, some bad — I was given on joining the business was some to the effect that all advertisements need to address one or other of three basic motivations: health, wealth and family happiness. This somewhat bleak and restricted view of human nature does nevertheless identify three important areas of motivation. To them it would now be sensible to add vanity, status, self-expression, fulfilment and anxiety. (I assume, of course, that protectiveness and love are covered by family happiness.) In the field of fund-raising I would certainly include the emotions of pity, anger, concern and sympathy.

I have often heard it said that raising funds for charity is the most difficult job that a writer can be given — the reason being that it involves persuading readers to part with money with-out receiving something in return.

I profoundly disagree. My belief is that anyone who makes a gift to charity secures in return something of great value: a satisfying sense of having helped others in need, or of having helped to save or preserve some part of a valuable heritage. In the case of medical charities there is also an obvious element of self interest, in that any of us, or other members of the family, could one day be beneficiaries of charity-funded medical research.

There are hundreds, if not thousands, of worthy organisations competing for the charitable buck. However generous the recipients of these appeals, they cannot possibly afford to respond to more than a fraction of them. Those which do secure a gift will be the ones which observe these simple rules for making successful appeals.

Establish a Need

Clearly the first thing that any appeal for funds must do is convince potential donors of a need, and arouse their sympathy. You have therefore to ensure that readers see clearly why the charity exists, and precisely which forms of pain, deprivation, distress or suffering it aims to prevent or alleviate . . . what threat it is trying to avert . . . which good cause it endeavours to promote . . . which vulnerable creatures need protection.

On the whole it is easier to engage people's interest, and arouse their sympathies, by focusing on the plight of individuals rather than of groups or categories . . . better to interest people in "victims of depression" by telling them about "Henry", or to tap people's anger about cruelty to animals by relating the story of how one creature was either harmed or helped. Threats to the environment — and indeed any conservation goal — are again easiest to picture in terms of specific examples.

Focus on People

Some of the most successful charity appeals are letters that focus sharply on real people — maybe some of those whom the charity exists to help, or an aid worker in the field. Potential donors find it easier to sympathise and empathise with the needs and predicaments of others than with abstractions and generalities. Instead of quoting a list of statistics ("x,000 people a year fall victim to glaucoma") or making general statements ("the scale of the problem is daunting as more and more of these people struggle to come to terms with their disability"), it is far more effective to introduce one glaucoma victim, and tell his story in such a way as to illustrate the awful reality of this affliction and its implications for his quality of life.

Ali is 59, but — worn down by the rigours of desert life — he looks ten years older. He is gradually losing his sight; without help he will, in less than six months, have become totally blind. In these harsh conditions, loss of sight can be a sentence of death for someone unable to fend for himself by tending the sparse crop, or drawing water from a distant well. His only hope is to make the arduous 80-mile journey to the small town of Kitu where we have established a small field ophthalmic unit where Ali can undergo a 15-minute operation to restore his sight. To guide him on this fateful pilgrimage, Ali has — not a dog — but his 11 year old grandson Meru. Holding on to the other end of his grandfather's stick, the boy is willing to help him make that journey. Will <u>you</u> help him — and others too? The cost of that life-saving operation is only £15. More than 400 others in the region are in the same plight as Ali.

The principles on which successful fund-raising appeals are based are summed up in a letter that I wrote to a charity that funds clubs for under-privileged young people, who had sent me some of their mailing packages for criticism. The letter is reproduced below.

———————

"Successful fund-raising efforts are based on appeals to *emotion* — supported, wherever possible, by rational justifications for giving. The reader needs to be made to feel that he (or she) is responding to some real human need, giving a helping hand to deserving kids, rather than simply throwing money into some bottomless well.

"It seems to me that nothing like enough is made of the fact that ABC can mount a two-pronged appeal: there is the obvious emotional appeal of saving youngsters from the scrap heap, of giving them a better start in life and of providing for the under-privileged some of the benefits taken for granted by those more comfortably placed. This, I believe, is the primary motivation that the letters should address.

"But there is also an important rational appeal: money given now to help is a sound investment — helping to prevent kids becoming a charge on the taxpayer later, and reducing the risk of finding one of them breaking into your home. Very little of this comes across to me from the intro packages which strike me as somewhat cold and heartless. They cry out for a warm, personal letter rather than a computerised message.

"Turning to the renewal efforts, these strike me as failing to hit the right balance between appreciation of past donations and the establishment of an urgent need for more. I think donors need to be made to feel good about what they have given already, and persuaded that it has been put to good use. At the same time, they can't be permitted to rest on their laurels. So while *appreciation* is an important element, it has to be used as a springboard for explaining an urgent, current need — some significant goal that is almost, but not quite, within reach, and which the donor's generous response will help us to achieve.

"Another problem with renewals is striking the right balance between *problems* (still needing to be solved) and *achievements* (what your gifts have helped us to accomplish). At least one of these efforts leans so heavily on problems that it gives the impression that most of them are insoluble — an impression reinforced by the depressing assertion 'and conditions are getting worse!' — followed by more gloom about suicides, homicides etc. You have to leave a little room for optimism.

"To start (as one of these letters does) with the announcement that 'I have great news! ABC has just received a $1 million gift' seems an odd way to begin an appeal for someone's money! Particularly when the accompanying leaflet goes on to explain that the money has not actually been given, but simply represents the ceiling to a promise by a respected Foundation to double other people's gifts. To my mind, the discrepancy between these statements undermines the credibility of the appeal. It is also psychologically misconceived. Donors don't want to play second fiddle to a rich Foundation. A sounder approach would have been 'slash the cost (because gifts are tax deductible) and double the value (because of the Foundation's promise) of your gift'.

"The packages seem system-driven, in the sense that the computer printed slip is the only component, apart from the reply envelope. I find myself asking (in the words of the song!) "Is that all there is?" A few token facts and figures on the reverse of the slip are not, I suspect, enough to persuade even the most well-intentioned to part with hard earned money. Not only do I need to be made to feel good about giving — I want to see people who ask for my money working hard for it!"

Set a Target

People often feel that they are being asked to throw money into a bottomless pit. They like to be told how their money will be used. You don't necessarily need to focus on a single goal (although it often pays to do this if you can). The important thing is to say how much money you need, and what it will be used for.

We need £100,000 to save the church . . .

£5,000 to take fifty deprived children on a much-needed holiday . . .

£20,000 to buy a mammography machine that will enable us to screen 5,000 women every year and — by detecting problems early — save the lives of a significant number.

Establish Your Credentials

Don't just rattle a begging bowl — tell people what you have done. They are more likely to give to a charity that can point to a record of solid achievement.

With the £5,000 raised, we have been able to equip a new laboratory.

Already we have restored the precious gift of sight to
3,000 cataract victims; now we need £10,000 to train doc-
tors and nurses to save the sight of the X,000 villagers
stricken every year.

Say "Thank You"

The best prospects for a gift are, in ascending order of value,
those who have given to other charities, and those who have
previously contributed to yours. But a lot of charities keep
coming back for more without paying previous supporters the
elementary courtesy of thanking them for their generosity and
making clear how much it is appreciated.

With your help we have been able to open a new ward.

I'd like to tell you the heartening stories of William and
Mary — just two of the people in desperate need for whom
— with your generous help — we have been able to find
homes.

Because of the kindness that you have shown to victims of
this crippling disorder, I want you to be one of the first to
hear about our plans. I believe, too, that because of the interest you've shown in the fight against this illness, you
will welcome the opportunity to contribute to the new
training and rehabilitation centre that we hope soon to
open in Sutton.

When people have helped before they like to know that their
gift has been appreciated, and that it has been of significant assistance. It should be possible to convey this message in a way
that doesn't lead them to believe that the charity is awash with
money, or that all the significant objectives have already been
achieved.

Convince Them that Their Gift Will Make a Difference

People often feel so daunted by the scale of suffering, or the dimensions of a problem, that they feel that no gift which they can afford would be enough to make a difference. Give them reassurance.

> *So often in the face of need one feels powerless to help. It is hard to believe that any gift one can afford would have any significant impact on the problem. So please believe me when I tell you that any gift you care to send — no matter what its size — will be gratefully received and put to immediate use.*

Show that a Goal is Within Reach

Sometimes one receives a charity appeal that makes you feel utterly hopeless. It goes on at such length about famine, flood and pestilence that readers are tempted to switch off, thinking "Oy, oy — what a terrible world, and what awful times we live in". So be wary of too much whingeing — making readers' flesh creep with graphic pictures of too many horrors.

Try to strike a hopeful, positive note — ideally, if you can, conveying the impression that much has already been achieved and that a crucially important goal is now — with just a bit more help — "within our grasp".

> *The new wards have been built . . . the laboratories and operating theatres equipped. Now all we need to establish this state-of-the-art centre of excellence in Winchester is £X00,000 to fund the recruitment of high-calibre staff. With your help, we can have the hospital up and running within the next twelve months.*

Arouse Emotion

Successful fund-raising efforts appeal directly to *emotion*, because the dominant motives for giving to charity are emotional. This is still true in the case of gifts where there may be a strong element of self-interest — such, for example, as gifts to fund medical research. But of course having appealed to emotion it is usually sensible to go on to establish a rational case for giving. But never forget that the purse-strings are most readily loosened by emotion.

Not every charity seems to be aware of this, I should have thought, fairly obvious and elementary fact. I once wrote an appeal for a charity concerned with foreign aid. One of its senior staff — a doctor — had just returned from a region of Africa stricken by famine and drought, and his account of the people's plight was both graphic and moving. I therefore decided to write in the first person as if the appeal for help had been written by him — as in fact, to a large extent, it had been.

When I had finished the letter I happened to pass through my secretary's office and was disconcerted to see tears rolling down her cheeks. "Oh, it's just so sad!" she sobbed and I saw that she was in the middle of typing my letter. Heartened by this spontaneous tribute I posted it off to the client only to have it criticised on the grounds that it "exploited emotion". My none-too-diplomatic reply was "What the hell do you think fund-raising is about?"

Ask for "Action this Day"

Churchill was famous for writing notes demanding "action this day". Every charity appeal should do the same.

> The need is urgent, the cost of this life-saving operation small. Please will you help by making, now — today — the gift of sight to Ali or one of the 15,000 other cataract victims in the Province? Just post your cheque or postal order in the reply-envelope enclosed. And may I take this opportunity to thank you for your generosity?

Here are some examples of fund-raising letters:

> Dear Supporter, You have, I know, been generous with help for our fight against this dread disease. That's why

you are one of the first to receive a copy of our latest Report. This comes with our grateful thanks for your support — and you will, I hope, be heartened by the encouraging progress it describes.

The advances made could not have been achieved without your help, and the support of others like you. But, of course, in this crucial sector of the war on cancer there can be no standing still. Although some conquests have been made, the war is not yet won. And the worst time to relax our efforts would be now, when so much progress has been made — when there is a feeling among researchers that victory could soon be won.

So I'm writing now (I hope before your Christmas gift list is complete!) to ask if you will be generous enough to add one name to the list; please will you send a gift to help our vital research?

I know that, in times like these, many people cannot afford to give as freely as they would wish. But I can promise you that _any_ sum, large or small, that you care to send will be much appreciated and put immediately to effective use.

We are committed to spending next year, on cancer research, a total of £x million. This is a sizeable sum by any standards. But investment on this scale is essential if we are to follow up all the promising lines of research now open to us. And to raise such a sum we shall need the help and goodwill of every well wisher.

This letter started with a "thank you". Let me end it with a "please"; please send *now* whatever sum you feel you can afford. Just detach the slip at the foot of this letter and post it with your gift.

I should like to take this opportunity to wish you — and all those close to you — a happy Christmas and a healthy and prosperous New Year.

Yours sincerely,

PS: Fight cancer with a "Christmas box". A traditional feature of the Christmas season is the custom of giving a "Christmas box" to those whom we consider, for one reason or another, to deserve one. What more deserving recipient could you possibly imagine than cancer research?

May I therefore make a suggestion? Put an empty box or carton by the telephone or on your dressing table. Fill it with any coins that you can spare from your small change . . . 20p, 50p or £1 pieces. When the box is full take the contents to your local building society or bank and send a cheque for that amount to help cancer research.

MAKE YOUR MONEY GO FURTHER THIS CHRISTMAS

Give pleasure to your friends <u>and</u> help mentally
handicapped children.

Dear Reader,
With Christmas only a few weeks away, you may find it rewarding to spend a few minutes looking through our latest catalogue, which provides an opportunity to do some rewarding Christmas shopping in the comfort of your home. You will find that this is a specially worthwhile way of shopping, because the money you spend goes further here than it would in any shop — buying pleasure for your friends <u>and</u> helping mentally handicapped children.

This is a pressing need to which we are wholeheartedly committed. You see, the disabilities of these children — which range from emotional disturbance or Downs Syndrome to severe brain damage — have deprived them of so much that, happily, other children take for granted. As if any one of these afflictions was not a burden heavy and cruel enough for one small soul to carry through life, some of these children suffer multiple disabilities. Others have never known the warmth and feeling of security that the close presence and support of a loving family can provide, having been totally rejected by their parents.

Perhaps, like us, you feel that it would be difficult to ask too much on behalf of such children. But I do not now ask for charity. All I ask is that you do some of your Christmas shopping from our catalogue.

As you will see the prices compare very favourably with those quoted in the shops. It costs you no more to shop this way, and your money works much harder — helping children in great need as well as buying Christmas presents.

You will find an order form attached to this letter, and a second one inside the catalogue for later use, or maybe to pass on with the catalogue to a friend.

Please use them to translate good intentions into action now.

Yours sincerely,

PLEASE JOIN WITH ME IN LEAVING OUR DESCENDANTS A PRICELESS BEQUEST

Dear Reader,

Some time ago I came across a cartoon that made me smile. It showed a family met to hear the reading of a will. "To my children", their lawyer reads aloud from the document before him, "I bequeath all the wonders of nature . . . the beauty of earth and sea and sky — of woods and meadows, and the creatures which inhabit them"!

For me, the joke has a sting in the tail which I am sure was not intended. For it is based on an assumption which is no longer valid: an assumption that the wonders of nature are certain to survive. And that therefore to mention them in a will can only be absurd — the empty, ridiculous gesture of one who has nothing worthwhile to bequeath.

Unfortunately, nothing could be further from the truth. For the fact is that some of the wonders of nature — among them, birdlife — will not survive for the enjoyment of future generations unless we take positive, urgent steps to protect them <u>now</u>. At the moment, we still have a great deal to leave our descendants. Though depleted, this country's resources of birdlife are still considerable. But this is an asset that could waste away unless we take steps to protect it.

And because I know that you share my concern for birdlife I am writing to ask you to join with me in saving this priceless bequest — a bequest that only we can safeguard for future generations.

The number of species which once flourished — and whose foothold here is now precarious -shows that birdlife is indeed an inheritance that is in jeopardy. At this very moment there are no less than x species whose survival is in danger — among them the Avocet, the Snowy Owl and the Osprey — all at the moment surviving (though as yet precariously) under this Society's protection.

But unless we continue our efforts — you and I, and others like us — our children, and their children, are going to lose part of their birthright. Their loss would be enormous, grievous -and irreplaceable. And it will have been our fault.

Frankly, this is not a load that I would care to have on my conscience. Birdlife has given me such pleasure that I can't bear the thought that young members of my family could be deprived of such enjoyment through any fault of mine. I should like a better memorial than a world in which these creatures are curiosities located only in museums. And I am sure that you would, too.

To protect our birdlife is the task to which we are dedicated. But we do need money. Money to buy land where dwindling species can find safe and permanent refuge. Money, above all, to educate people so that more become aware of the need to accept responsibility for protecting these treasures of nature.

Imagine a landscape shorn of all the colour, sounds and movement contributed by birdlife. Without birds to give it life the countryside would be dead. And if, as I hope, you would like future generations to inherit something better than a dead and silent landscape you can -with the stroke of a pen — make a bequest that will benefit not only your descendants, but the nation as a whole. A bequest of the kind I am suggesting would cost you nothing in your lifetime. I am asking you to remember this Society in your will.

No doubt, like me, you have made a will whose principal provisions have been thoughtfully framed to take account of the beneficiaries' urgent needs. Now you have it within your power to add to these bequests something of incalculable value: a country whose resources of birdlife you have helped to save for their enjoyment.

Just in case you would like to help us in this way, I enclose a draft letter that you might care to sign and send to your lawyer. It simply puts into legal language a bequest that I am sure you'd wish to make to future generations. It is, believe me, a legacy that they will value.

Could a modest sum of money buy you a more enduring, valuable memorial?

Yours sincerely,

PS: So that we may thank you properly for your generosity, I should be most grateful if you could return in the reply paid envelope provided the enclosed card giving details of any legacy you might care to make.

"A little fellow feeling makes us wondrous kind", and by far the best prospect for an appeal for funds is somebody who has first-hand experience — as victim, carer, friend or relative — of whatever disability or misfortune the charity exists to do something about.

Dear

"O wad some Pow'r the giftie gie us to see oursels as others see us!" wrote Scotland's greatest poet. But one group of people knows only too well how acutely distressing and humiliating it can be to see yourself through the eyes of others. Job applicants with a history of mental illness soon learn to see themselves through the eyes of potential employers — quickly grow to recognise the signs of fear, suspicion and hostility that is the common lot of those who try to get back to work, following a mental illness.

If you heard of somebody made redundant, or compelled to take early retirement, your instant reaction would I am sure be one of sympathy — you would want to do something to help.

I am writing to ask for your help in securing employment for those made redundant, not by an employer, but by society — for people compelled to retire early, without compensation, not late in their careers, but often in their prime and even in their youth — rejected for paid (and sometimes even voluntary) employment purely because they have had the misfortune to suffer mental illness.

Many of those who are thrown onto the social scrapheap so unjustly, so cruelly and so early have valuable knowledge, experience and skills which makes their rejection by employers not only cruel but tragically wasteful.

Let me tell you, by way of example, the experience of just three former patients (Brief case histories)

Few of us manage to get through life without encountering, once or twice, the sharp pain of rejection. But for the former mental patient looking for a job, the harsh experience of rejection is continuous. Repeatedly turned down for no better reason than prejudice or mis-conception about the nature of their illness, they lose all confidence in themselves. Repeated rejection is tragically destructive of morale. As one of them puts it, "the one thing that all of us long for is to be <u>accepted</u>".

<u>Symbol of personal value</u>
For those of us lucky enough to have one, a job symbolises our individual value to society (what they do for a living is one of the first things that we want to know about people). This is why denial of employment rots a person's self-esteem, producing in time a feeling of despairing worthlessness. If, as I hope, you have a good opinion of yourself — a favour-able "self-image" — it probably rests to a significant extent on the job you do in the family or the community.

As a thanks offering for your job, for your sense of personal value, please send now as much as you can afford to help our campaign for the mentally ill and handicapped — particularly for those who seek the fulfilment of a job.

Yours sincerely

_____

AN URGENT AND PERSONAL INVITATION TO JOIN IN THE WAR AGAINST CANCER

Dear Reader,
If you have ever been shocked to learn that a relative or friend has cancer your immediate reaction was probably to ask "How can <u>I</u> help?"

I should like in this letter to try to give you an answer to that question, and explain how you can make a significant personal contribution to the war on cancer.

Concern and sympathy

The concern and sympathy that we all feel for cancer victims is an instinctive, generous response that demands some practical expression. And, if you can't always give them your personal care and attention, there is, nevertheless, a lot that you can do to help — not only cases known to you, but also those whom you may know only as statistics.

Sobering figures

And those statistics are alarming. One in every four of the population of this country will, at some time in their lives, be diagnosed as suffering from cancer. And even despite the tremendous strides of recent years in both prevention and treatment, cancer is still the cause of one death in every five.

A personal stake in success

Sobering figures like these make it clear that the war against cancer is not only a battle fought on behalf of others. For the fact is that it is a campaign in which everyone has a personal stake — a war which, although perhaps first declared on behalf of others, may in the end prove to be one in which victory becomes an urgent, personal priority.

Where your help is needed

And among the forces now fighting this battle, none are more heavily, extensively or successfully engaged than us. Our army of researchers has already made a major contribution to the advances in treatment that I mentioned earlier. Thanks to the dedicated efforts of those engaged in both research and treatment, a diagnosis of cancer is no longer a sentence of death. Many forms of the disease, if diagnosed early enough, can now be cured.

Importance of early diagnosis

But although much hard-won progress has been made, a great deal still remains to be learned. There is, alas, just not space in this letter to tell you about all the promising and exciting projects that we are currently financing. But what I can tell you is that the war on cancer is being waged on many major fronts.

Resources urgently needed

As in any war, the costs of waging it are heavy. But never, surely, have there been so many worthwhile war aims; and never before has victory been so great a prize — a goal for which so many millions of people hope and pray.

Please, please help us to seize that prize. With your help, the battle can — and, one day we know <u>will</u> — be won. Your gift will help to bring V-Day closer . . . Help to answer all those prayers.

Large or small, your gift will be gratefully received, and — you can be certain — put immediately to the best possible use. But you might like to know that, for the reasons explained on the back of the form enclosed with this letter, a gift made by Deed of Covenant is particularly welcome because we can reclaim for our research the income tax paid by you on the amount of your gift. So a Deed of Covenant offers one way to increase the value of your gift to help cancer research, without any extra cost to you.

But whatever the size and the form of your gift, I urge you — no, I <u>beg</u> you — to lose no time in helping us to win what is probably the greatest battle of our time.

Yours sincerely,

Chapter 12

Political Persuasion

Contrary to what they themselves seem to believe, politicians are seldom accomplished practitioners of the art of persuasion. One of the more dispiriting features of any election campaign are the letters from candidates that flutter through one's letterbox.

The obligatory "election address" sets out to offer reasons why a particular candidate should be elected. These letters ring about as true as a cracked wine glass. Any commercial organisation whose sales letters were couched in such complacent terms would soon be out of business. Even the candidates' speeches carry more conviction than their letters.

Essentially, an election manifesto is a selling document whose composition can be speeded and assisted by following the advice given elsewhere in this book on writing letters and brochures. Such copywriting levers as Empowerment, Promise and Challenge are every bit as relevant and powerful in a political context. So too are the techniques for projecting an image of the writer as a likeable, trustworthy and honest individual — rather than a political glove puppet terrified of departing by a hair's breadth from the party line.

Instead of a letter or manifesto that concentrates in a credible fashion on the potential benefits of voting in a certain way, too many election communications seem to take the form of a photograph of the candidate with a smile that registers about 9 on the Richter Scale flanked by his wife and 2.4 children, along-

side the less than compelling information that he has lived in
the constituency for many years, is a member of Rotary and the
Lions, and enjoys a game of golf.

In place of the usual stilted and clichéd communication so
familiar to voters, a letter along the lines of the sample below
that succeeded in giving a flavour of the candidate's personality, conveying a picture of somebody with passion and convic-
tions who if elected would do his level best to deliver benefits
— and who at the same time is realistic and honest enough to
admit that not everything lies within the control of politicians —
might command more interest and respect.

> Soon now you will have an opportunity to decide who you
> want to represent you in (whatever) for the next five
> years.
>
> And if you will kindly allow me a few minutes of your time,
> I shall try in this letter to explain why I think it will be in
> your own and your family's interests to cast your vote for
> me and for the party that I represent.
>
> The process of voting at any election is so familiar that it
> can be easy to under-estimate the opportunity that it pro-
> vides. So may I make a suggestion? — Try for a moment to
> look beyond the routine process of marking a cross beside
> a name, and see your vote for what it really is: an oppor-
> tunity for you to influence decisions and events which,
> over the next few years, will have a crucial impact on your
> own and your family's life.
>
> . . . How long you are obliged to wait for an urgent opera-
> tion — and the quality of the treatment when you get it.
> How much of your hard-earned money is snatched away
> in taxes. . . . The likelihood of being robbed or burgled . . .
> the degree of job security that you have . . . the size of
> pension you are likely to have in retirement — and the
> quality of education that young people in your family will

receive. To say nothing of how much the money in your pocket is able to buy.

. . . These are issues that concern every one of us. And rather than take up your time with a lot of sententious, high-sounding waffle about the aims and policies of the party to which I belong, I'd like to tell you about the personal priorities that decided me to become a candi-date, and which — more than any considerations of party solidarity — will shape the way that I cast my vote on your behalf if I am elected.

You will note that I stress <u>priorities</u> rather than policies and aims. This is because, however well intentioned and seductive a policy may sound, you and I both know that scope to implement it may turn out to be severely limited by economic forces that lie beyond any government's control. At the end of the day, what government is all about is deciding which of many desirable objectives shall have priority in the allocation of available resources.

So let me tell you my personal priorities. I am convinced that economic health depends on maintaining the high level of employment. Perhaps, however, you share my suspicion of politicians who offer promises of jobs. Jobs are created, not by governments, but by <u>employers</u>. And in my view the most that any government can do is provide the right conditions for individual employers to prosper, grow and generate more jobs.

This in turn means lifting off their backs the costs and frustrations of bureaucratic over-regulation, such as currently afflicts most of our European neighbours. We need a flexible labour market in which workers can move freely, and employers are not deterred from expanding by the crippling costs of paying — on top of high wages — a mounting toll of statutory welfare charges.

Since it is not governments but taxpayers — that is, you and me — who provide the resources to fight crime, provide decent pensions and help those in need, I believe very strongly in directing help where it is needed most. I see no point in paying social benefits to people who don't really need them, nor in subsidising fraudulent claims for benefit to the tune of billions of pounds (while I am all for being 'tough on crime' I am even more strongly in favour of being tough on criminals — and that includes benefit cheats).

The goal of directing funds where they will do most good has important implications too for the National Health Service. Modern medical treatment is hugely costly, and the cost of effective treatment for some serious conditions is now so high that many of the victims are being denied life-saving treatments on financial grounds. What this means is that, in order to be able to continue free delivery to all of a mediocre service treating commonplace conditions, some patients with grave life-threatening disorders are effectively sentenced to death.

Perhaps you share my belief that this is indefensible, and my readiness to devote a larger share of the NHS budget to ensure that no patients are denied the life-saving treatment that they so desperately need.

Turning to the future of young people, my view has always been that the function of a school is to equip them with a measurable mastery of such basic skills as reading, writing and arithmetic. I would crack down on any school that squandered scarce resources on teachers who sacrifice their pupils' needs on the altar of self-indulgent, fashionable academic theories of education.

Before casting your vote for one of the candidates, you might well wish to know the views of each of us on what is probably the most important issue of our time. I mean of course the question of whether or not the United Kingdom should join the single European currency.

And here — whatever my party's official policy may be — I am quite certain of my own position. If a referendum were to be held today, my vote would be an emphatic 'No'.

While I am all for membership of an economic and social community of European States, I do not favour the surrender of our hard-won independence that would be the unpleasant consequence of allowing sterling to be absorbed into an untested, unproved "Euro", with consequences, both for jobs and for our social and economic health that could prove catastrophic.

There you have it then — a full and candid statement of my personal priorities. And the reason why I am a member of this party is because I am certain that its historic instincts and beliefs — as well as its current leadership and composition — bring its policies closest to my values and beliefs. If these happen to coincide with yours, I feel justified in asking for your vote.

I can promise you that, if elected, I shall always strive to represent, to the best of my ability, the interests of <u>all</u> constituents.

Yours sincerely,

Maybe politicians attach a bit too much importance to indirect persuasion in the shape of "spinning" the presentation of "news", and not enough to overt attempts to influence voters through websites, letters, manifestos and party political broadcasts. If they chose words more carefully, assembled them with greater skill, and wrote or spoke them as if they actually meant something and were backed by some emotion more substantial than a desperate desire to get elected, maybe politics as a trade would be held in more respect and its practitioners would be better liked.

At present, too many of them come across in print as cardboard figures, cut out at party headquarters, and in speech as ventriloquist's dummies mouthing platitudes dictated by a pager.

The qualities in which most attempts at political persuasion seem conspicuously deficient are those of sincerity, conviction and credibility — all even more crucial in a political than in a commercial context. Only a singularly stupid and complacent copywriter could fail to be aware that advertising claims are viewed with scepticism. Why is it, then, that so many politicians do not yet seem to grasp the hostility and disbelief aroused by their promises and pledges — the contempt in which their partisan complacency is held?

To politicians seeking to make contact with voters' minds, rather than their waste bins, I would (perhaps presumptuously) commend the advice offered in other chapters of this book, not least in those on the copywriting sins and graces. After all, the motivations into which they are attempting to tap are some of the strongest known to man, including the traditional big three that I mentioned earlier — Health, Wealth and Family Happiness.

Chapter 13

Virtues and Vices

The Seven Copywriting Graces

Before examining the Seven Deadly Sins of copywriting (we'll come to these in the next section) let's take a look at the virtues — qualities to prize in a copywriter and in any piece of copy. We'll call these the Seven Graces (I know that in classical mythology there were only three Graces, but in copywriting there are seven).

1. Authority

Some copy — unhappily, far too little — possesses a quality that is easier to recognise than to define or describe. Whether you call it pizzazz, relish or panache it is quite unmistakable when you come across it and helps to lift any piece of copy, however mundane or common-place the product, to a higher level of persuasiveness, authority and credibility. Reading it is like watching a consummate actor dominate the stage, or an ace sportsman running rings around his rivals. For examples, see the descriptions of premiums on pages 133 to 137 and the fund-raising appeals on pages 175 to 189.

Given some commonplace product to promote, or some intrinsically unexciting proposition, the copywriter's job is to seize it by the scruff of its neck and, by skilfully applying creative cosmetics, send it out into the marketplace looking fresh and appealing. This is not a skill that can easily be taught by any training course that Human Resources departments can devise. It can only be acquired by somebody with writing talent and creative energy who has listened with appropriate attention to the candid criticism of professional superiors.

This quality of Authority is often the product of painstaking research, evident where the writer knows what he is talking about because he has taken the trouble to research the subject thoroughly and therefore succeeds in communicating his knowledge to the reader.

2. Empathy

One of the most valuable attributes of a copywriter is the ability to stand in other people's shoes — approaching what he has to sell from the reader's point of view. This is often made quite difficult by the well-meant efforts of marketing, brand and product managers, who — lacking the imagination to see their product from the user's point of view — tend to be obsessed with the minutiae of product specification — features of it that can be listed and measured. If they had their way — and with the support of the engineers and designers responsible for it — the product would be sold with the help of a letter and brochure that was largely a glorified checklist — a specification spiced with boastful adjectives.

The reader on the other hand is interested, less in what has gone into the product, than in what he will get out of it. The difference in perspective is crucial to making a sale and one of the key roles of the copywriter is to act as an interpreter — looking at everything from the reader's point of view, and presenting every product feature as a user benefit.

The importance of this difference in perspective is for me epitomised in the old aphorism about the customer who buys a drill: "He doesn't want a ½ inch drill — he wants a ½ inch hole!"

Some of the most persuasive copy that I've read was for do-it-yourself equipment. To my certain knowledge the writer was a hopeless handyman — incapable even of putting up a shelf or hammering a nail in straight. (In his household, such tasks had to be undertaken by his wife.) Nevertheless he had the ability to empathise with the kind of competent handyman that he would himself have loved to be and to present the product in persuasive terms.

Occasionally, what you have to sell provides an opportunity that it would be foolish not to grasp to show the reader that you understand his emotions, needs and problems. You then of course go on to link them with your product.

> Dear Reader,
> If you've ever had a houseplant look sick or die on you, for no reason you could discover . . . wanted to take a cutting for a friend, but hesitated through fear of harming the plant . . . wondered whether some exotic species could possibly flourish in <u>your</u> home . . . or waited (and waited!) for that African Violet to flower again . . . here's a book on indoor gardening that solves all the problems you've ever met — or are ever likely to meet.

Or suppose that you are trying to sell a language course:

> When you can't speak the language of the country, you are effectively tongue-tied — cut off from most of the people you meet. This is true of both social and business situations. On social occasions, inability to speak or understand the language can make one feel like a shy child at a party. Everyone around you seems to be having a fine time, and getting along like a house on fire, while you are forced to stand there silent and embarrassed. For all practical purposes lack of any language skills limits your choice of destinations for a holiday.
>
> While I won't pretend that our language courses will equip you to write novels or make speeches in the language, I can guarantee that they will, within a few weeks, make it possible for you to get by in the language and get on with the people that you meet.

Often no more than a thin line separates a vague wish from a powerful desire. Skilful copywriters find a way to fan the flame and, having sparked a wish, coax it gently into the flame of desire. For example, a vague, barely-formed ambition to learn a foreign language is something that many people harbour. By making them feel *deprived* — as in the example above — you can help them to perceive it as a need.

The key to selling your phrase-book or language guide is to use images that help people to perceive it as a bridge between inadequacy or deprivation and a richer, fuller life.

3. Euphony

A sensitivity to *euphony* — the rhythm of the words and sentences he writes, is one of the attributes of a competent writer. The rhythm created by skilful choice and positioning of words and phrases enhances readability, reinforces the meaning of a message and makes it easier to understand and remember.

This is particularly true of headlines. Compare these two claims for a language course:

Learn German or French in six months

Learn French or German in six months

Both use exactly the same words. But the second makes a stronger headline simply because it has greater euphony — the rhythm of the words is better when they are arranged in this sequence.

As you write or read, listen with an inner ear to the rhythm of the words, using it to rein-force the meaning of your message.

4. Sincerity and
5. Credibility

The qualities in which so much copy seems to me deficient are precisely those that oil the wheels of any form of communication between people: they include humanity, a touch of humour, liveliness, *believability*. So my next nominations for the Copywriting Graces are the qualities of *Sincerity* and *Credibility*, evident in these extracts from a letter written to sell a book about the use of English:

> Dear Reader,
> When I tell you that something you use every day could be put to better use . . . and that using it better could help you to win greater influence, more respect and higher status — promotion and a larger income . . . widen your circle of friends and possibly even gain you fame and power . . . you might well be curious to know what that "something" is.
>
> . . . It is in fact the English language; and knowing how to use it well — in writing and in speech — has won for others all the things I've mentioned.
>
> <u>It could do the same for you</u>. A new book, just published, provides a golden key to the effective use of language which could open new doors for you in your career and social life, and (if you have children) get them off to a better start in their careers.
>
> I shall not pretend that the book will turn you overnight into a best-selling novelist, a nationally-famous columnist, or a successful politician. What it will do is equip you with some of the basic skills of professional communi-cators such as journalists and politicians.
>
> And if you're wondering what need you and others in your family have of such skills, you have only to look for a moment at the kind of world in which we live: a world in which educational progress, success at work and social satisfaction depend to a large extent on the power to communicate effectively in writing and in speech.

6. Humanity

My next nomination for the Graces is *Humanity* — a deft and
human touch with words that succeeds in establishing the
writer as a friendly, likeable, trustworthy individual.

> Dear Customer,
> You probably know that old Latin tag "in vino veritas". It
> may be no more than the result of generously sampling
> our own stock, but I find that most people in the wine
> trade <u>are</u> refreshingly truthful.
>
> One does not, for example, find on the lists of reputable
> merchants the kind of inflated, patently untruthful prose
> that appears on some restaurant menus (which so often
> owe more to the art of the copywriter than to the skill of
> the chef!)
>
> You know the kind of thing: "Made from succulent white
> grapes, morning-gathered while the gentle dew still glis-
> tens on their skins, and trodden by the dainty feet of village
> maidens fresh from their morning ablutions in a nearby
> mountain stream"! Mercifully, there are few wine merchants
> who inflict this sort of rubbish on their customers.
>
> My belief has always been that the description of a wine
> should be both brief and candid — written, not to per-
> suade, but to <u>inform</u>. People's tastes vary, and few wines
> are perfect. To describe every bottle on one's list in the
> reverent terms appropriate to a first-growth claret is not, I
> believe, the right way to sell wine. You might make one
> sale, but customers would be unlikely to return for more.
> And it is on repeat sales to <u>satisfied</u> customers that every
> sound business is founded.
>
> I believe that people should be able to trust their wine
> merchant as completely as their lawyer or their doctor.
> (Indeed, if half what one reads in the papers is true, more
> people might be in better health and circumstances if they

had only spent on wine the sums disbursed on medication
or on litigation!)

7. Likeability

And here's some letter copy that exhibits the precious quality
of *Likeability*, the seventh of the Graces.

> Dear Member,
> In more robust days when a tot of rum was every sailor's
> birthright, and the mainbrace was spliced every day, that
> potent red spirit became an unofficial currency. Rum in the
> Royal Navy was, literally, a "liquid asset" — borrowed by
> the improvident and lent (at appropriate rates of interest)
> by the cunning or the thrifty.
>
> As I recall it, the currency had two denominations —
> known as "sippers" and "gulpers". And here perhaps I
> should explain that these terms referred (if I may put it
> that way) not to the drinker, but rather to the drunk — ie
> to the size of the tot, and not to the person drinking it . . .
> "sippers" being a fairly modest mouthful, and "gulpers" a
> swallow of generous size.
>
> Though coined in connection with a spirit, I have often
> thought these terms appropriate to wine — not so much as
> measure, but as some indication of type. Both terms strike
> me as more helpful than many of the more pretentious
> categorisations that the wine trade uses. (Who, for exam-
> ple, would not find "sippers" a better indication of quality
> in clarets than the pompous, and now largely outdated,
> classification into First and Second Growths. And who,
> finding a new wine described as a "gulper", could fail to
> understand that what is on offer is not a fine wine to be
> sipped and savoured, but an agreeable, "moreish" and ob-
> viously less-costly wine which it would be appropriate to
> quaff with relish.

> Well, believing quality and variety to be the keys to good
> selection, I offer this month a case that includes both "sip-
> pers" and "gulpers".

In addition to the Graces, two other qualities are often present
in good copy: one is *immediacy*, the other *realism*. Such qualities help to lift the product out of the bland, twilight never-
never land of advertising and thrust it at the reader as a recognisable slice of real life:

> Dear Reader,
> You are driving along, not a care in the world, when sud-
> denly buildings appear. A roadside sign shows that you
> are entering the limits of a town. In no time at all you are
> assailed on all sides by directions and instructions: "ONE-
> WAY STREET" . . . "TOWN CENTRE" . . . "NO PARKING!" . . .
> "NEW ROAD LAYOUT AHEAD". Lights flash, horns honk,
> bells ring, and sirens blare.
>
> A nightmare? — Yes. It is also the everyday experience of
> motorists entering a strange town.
>
> So here, to calm your nerves and guide you swiftly,
> smoothly to your destination, is a new book of up-to-the-
> minute town-plans for motorists.

And here's another example from a letter about that book on
English usage:

> Every day in a vast range of situations — social, domestic
> and business — our powers of self-expression are being
> put to the test, and a lot can depend on how well we rise
> to the challenge, because (as so many foreigners have dis-
> covered) English is a language that is full of traps for the
> unwary.
>
> Take, for example, that crucial first step towards landing a
> really good job: the letter one writes to apply for it. What's
> the best way to begin — something conventional but

stilted ("I write in response to your advertisement . . .") or is it better to risk an off-beat, but striking, beginning?

Or suppose that you are faced with the need to write a letter of condolence. This book shows you, with striking examples, how best to express the sympathy you feel — the sense of loss you share — in a way that offers some consolation to the reader without sounding mawkish, insincere or sentimental.

And on the subject of telephoning — something you do every day — how good are you at projecting yourself to people who can't see you? This book explains how to put in your voice the unseen expression on your face — the smile of pleasure, the frown of anger, the sceptical lift of an eyebrow. For the swift and dramatic improvement that it can bring to your telephone manner alone, the book is worth many times its modest price.

The Seven Deadly Copywriting Sins

In the previous section we looked at several examples of good copy and at the qualities to look for in good promotion copy. Since one can learn as much from vices as from virtues let's turn now to the characteristic flaws and weaknesses of ineffective copy. These I would further classify as two fatal maladies, and seven deadly sins.

Two maladies are fatal to good copy: the first is *Graphomania*, a morbid desire to fill the page with words — to go on writing way beyond the average individual's propensity or willingness to read.

For the curse of direct response writing is an amiable delusion among some writers that, because they have gone to the trouble of *writing* copy, the recipient has some sort of obligation to read it, however boring it may be.

The second malady is related to the first, but is quite distinct: I would describe it as adjectival logorrhoea — by which I mean never using one adjective when you can think of three;

never putting, in a single sentence, what can be spun out to four; rambling on for three paragraphs when one would have been enough. I mean this kind of thing:

A very special, limited, introductory offer.

An exciting, once-in-a-lifetime, money-saving opportunity.

Handy protective, transparent, plastic, navigating wallet.

The seven deadly sins of copywriting are, in my view, as follows:

1. Unreadability

The first is unreadability, for it is surely axiomatic that the first duty of any writer is to get his copy *read*.

Here's an example of copy that flouts just about every rule for making copy readable:

And for every one of these areas travel experts have planned a separate, self-contained motoring tour — a fascinating ROUTE designed to link up, in leisurely, relaxed, carefree motoring, the loveliest beauty spots and the most interesting places and sights the region can offer — a ROUTE which sets out to capture the unique 'character', the true 'flavour' of the area . . . the history and legends of the past as well as the day-to-day life, work, arts, crafts and customs of the local people you will meet on your motoring travels today!

It is, I think, salutary to bear in mind a couplet from Byron's *Don Juan*:

Society is now one polished horde,
Formed of two mighty tribes, the Bores and Bored.

I sometimes think that copywriters are over-represented in the ranks of the Bores and that too many of their mailing pieces are driving customers into that other mighty tribe, the Bored.

Another copywriting vice is *being too demanding* — over-taxing the reader's goodwill, patience, intellect or time. It is sometimes helpful to think of the recipient of a letter as someone who is powered by a very weak battery — easily exhausted by any undue effort he's obliged to make to grasp your message.

If you imagine a scale of comprehension, calibrated from zero to 100, the reader is at zero when his eye lights on a piece of copy. In the brief time available you have to try and shift the reader as far as possible across the scale before that battery is exhausted. To do this you need to use all the skill and guile at your command to attract attention, hold it, and punch across your message.

The process of writing almost any piece of copy is summed up in a useful mnemonic which also happens to be the title of an opera by Verdi:

AIDA

The first A stands for *Attention*. Your copy has first to *grab* attention. The I stands for *Interest*. Having secured the reader's attention your copy has to gain — and hold — his *interest*. D is for *Desire*. Does your copy stimulate desire — does it make the reader itch to get his hands on what you offer? In this connection it is useful to recall Carlisle's Rule of Acquisition: "The purchase of any product can be rationalised if the desire to own it is strong enough." And the final A is for *Action*. Does the copy have enough clarity and urgency to overcome inertia, and impel the reader to reply?

So go through what you have written and *edit ruthlessly*. Look for passages where you have used more words than necessary. Look for long, multi-syllabic words for which an adequate one-syllable synonym exists. Look for long sentences that can be broken into short ones. Look for examples of the passive rather than the active voice. Bear in mind (Sydney) Smith's Writing Rule:

> In composing, as a general rule, run your pen through every other word you have written; you have no idea what the vigour it will give your style.

2. Self-centredness

My nomination for the Second Deadly Sin would be Self-centredness. A lot of copy is appallingly self-centred. It presents the product, or the offer, from the writer's, or from the vendor's, point of view — instead of (as, of course, it should) looking at them through the reader's eyes. How's this for a self-centred opening paragraph?

> Dear Smoker,
> What a magnificent season it has been so far for the Rothmans Rally Team. Getting off to a superb start, they won the prestigious Monte Carlo Rally outright and are still leading the challenge for the World Rally Championship title.

3. Self-indulgence

The next sin is Self-indulgence. This is copy where the writer is on an ego-trip — demonstrating his own cleverness, and what he fondly imagines to be literary virtuosity. This kind of thing is sometimes known irreverently as "Copywriter's Stately". What is wrong with it is, of course, that the writer gets between the reader and the product. Like this:

> Dear Reader,
> How could you possibly enjoy 'Kidnapped' unless you are eager for the groaning of a sailing ship's timbers and the creaking of her lines . . . for a taste of salt spray in the breeze . . . and for the rise and fall of the horizon as the ship glides from the crest of one wave to another.

Another aspect of self-indulgence is verbosity. Writers who fail to edit their copy as sharply as they should over-tax the reader's patience, dutifully rehearsing all the reasons for buying a product with the relentless, obsessive egocentricity of a hypochondriac telling you his symptoms, with no twitch or twinge, no ache or pain allowed to pass unmentioned.

4. Implausibility

The Fourth Deadly Sin is Implausibility. Desperate to shift their product, some writers make frankly incredible claims — recklessly promising the reader more than the massed distilleries of Scotland could be able to deliver — more than all the world's breweries and pill-pushers have been able to supply — in the shape of instant, beatific, lasting happiness. How's this for implausible copy?

> And, as a final touch of greatness, these volumes have been collected for you in an opulent, new edition that proudly bears the splendour of the 'Czar Nicholas' style binding. These exquisite volumes will enrich your home with the grandeur of old St Petersburg, and will be passed from generation to generation with unflagging pride.

Remember that because you've an interest in making a sale, it doesn't by any means follow that the reader is interested in making a purchase: you have to work to capture that interest. And the way to do this is not to bludgeon him with boastful, implausible claims. Charged with selling some humble gizmo, some useful but undramatic widget, it is unwise to promote it in terms that would be more appropriate to the offer of a tablet which, at minuscule cost, will turn water into wine or gasoline.

So beware of empty boasts, exaggerated claims and all the flatulent puffery that marks third-rate copy.

On the subject of credibility, let me remind you of Raper's Rule: "Don't claim too much. The manufacturer of hair restorer never advertises that it will grow hair on the back of the neck."

5. Exaggeration

As we saw earlier, a lot of the copy in sweepstakes promotions is overly reliant on an element of exaggeration. Who has not at some time or another received a mailing whose implausible flavour is captured by this parody? It illustrates the kind of Exaggeration that is my nomination for the Fifth Deadly Sin.

> Dear Mr Mascarpone,
> This is an exciting day for the whole Mascarpone household: the arrival at 14 Gorgonzola Villas of an exciting Official Million Dollar Winning Opportunity Affidavit and Sweepstakes Entry Deposition, made out personally in the name of Mascarpone and individually addressed to 14 Gorgonzola Villas.
>
> Not everyone in Tuscany will be lucky enough to receive this magnificent 2000 (TWO THOUSAND) words of overheated sweepstakes copy designed to convince them that they have already come triumphantly through 19 — yes, NINETEEN — of the 20 stages that there are to winning ONE MILLION DOLLARS (or $100 a year for life) in a draw that they have never heard of, let alone actually entered.
>
> Mr Mascarpone, I must ask you now to do something for me. I want you to gather the whole Mascarpone family round you for what will undoubtedly be the most important family conference that you have ever held — a decision how to spend money that you do not have and are never likely to get. Think about it, Mr Mascarpone: would you prefer to invest it for income and capital growth — perhaps in a business of your own, like a chain of massage parlours (offering tempting opportunities for you to combine business with pleasure!) or would you instead use the money to buy all the lottery tickets that your heart desires; with your winnings you could paper your whole house with lottery tickets and still have enough left over to lose another million dollars. This could be the biggest decision you will ever face. Discuss it with your family and then

> **when you have made up your mind just stick one of these**
> **Mascarpone Decision Stamps in one of the special decision**
> **boxes in your Winning Opportunity Affidavit.**

Much sweepstakes copy conveys a hidden message that even the dullest reader should be able to decipher. It runs like this:

> *We believe that you who are reading these words are so*
> *deprived and underprivileged that the arrival of a package*
> *of patronising and implausible junk mail will bring a daz-*
> *zling shaft of sunlight into your dull and empty life.*

6. Insensitivity

Far too much copy is embarrassingly insensitive. The fact that an advertiser has paid someone good money to write it, and spent a lot more to have it printed and mailed can only be explained in terms of a wholly mistaken belief that different rules apply to advertising copy than to any other form of reading matter. People buy newspapers for the way in which they present and analyse news . . . the tone of the comments they provide on issues of the day. They choose magazines for the nature and style of the contents — books for the authors' skill in providing the rewards they seek — enlightenment, amusement, excitement or whatever. What on earth persuades presumably hard-headed businessmen that people will volunteer to read effusions designed to sell them something that offers no kind of reward whatever to the reader — not even one as basic as a good read? The element of sensitivity is often conspicuously absent; all the copy offers is an arduous trudge through a mass of verbiage that dutifully but tediously visits every single boring feature of a totally commonplace product.

Certain words tend to crop up again and again with the wearisome predictability of the leaden clichés that real estate agents use so freely . . . "Benefits from" . . . "A wealth of beams" . . . "Well presented" . . . "Favoured position" and "Sought-after location". The copywriter's equivalents are "Exciting" (as in Opportunity or Introductory Offer) . . . "Invaluable" — a word that is usually applied to something of neither intrinsic value nor practical utility. The strong gravitational pull of fatuous hyperbole is apparent everywhere . . . "Marvellous" . . . "Fabulous" . . . "Wonderful" . . . "Unprecedented" . . . and all the rest. How many copywriters I wonder read with a critical, objective eye the claims that they make for a product and the terms in which they make them?

One reason why direct mail is perceived by so many as junk is that so much of it is, frankly, *boring* — written, not by a copywriter, but by a human word processor. Programme one of these with a product brief — or a list of product features — and the result will be a thousand or so words of dutiful but boring prose — flavourless, insensitive and difficult to read.

7. Illiteracy

Evidence of illiteracy in a copywriter can be as disconcerting as a bloodstained apron in the kitchen. It is therefore dismaying to find advertisements and mailing packages that are crammed with malapropisms, linguistic infelicities and crass grammatical errors. Here are just a few:

> As a valued customer, we are writing to you . . .

> The policy comprises of three main features . . .

> The book has three principle uses

> Explains the principals of successful gardening

> The quality of service has been increased

> A survey into . . .

> Less demands are being made

> . . . lessen the plight of . . .

There are countless similar litmus tests of literacy. A choice example takes the form of a correction often made to copy in which the word causal (meaning caused by) has been used by a writer. In the mistaken belief that this could only be a misprint, the letters are solemnly rearranged to read *casual* — a pattern more familiar to the illiterate who find nothing odd in a sentence that speaks of "a casual connection"!

A knowledge of elementary grammar is one of the cornerstones of education, and illiteracy should in my view be a firing offence for any copywriter. See how many errors you can spot in this short passage:

> As a valued and exacting customer with an eye for quality and value, we are pleased to be able to proudly make you this exciting offer. The result of a thorough survey into the preferences and needs of our customers, this fabulous mobile telephone with its unique and exclusive 'morning chorus' ringing tone that will fill your home with the welcome sounds of birdsong is sure to win you admiring and envious glances when friends and colleagues call you in a crowded railway carriage. And quite apart from its value as a fashion accessory, a mobile in the car will lessen the plight of any motorist marooned on a busy motorway (a principle source of anxiety for female drivers).

Appendix 1

Traps for the Unwary

Keeping Out of Trouble

To some direct marketers it comes as a disagreeable surprise to discover how many constraints — moral, social, ethical and legal — restrict a copywriter's freedom. When a communication happens to be commercial it is even easier to give offence than when it is political or social. Some people are so prone to take offence that they come more than half way to meet you, often reading into what you have written some offensive implication that may not have been intended. So it is wise to bear in mind as you write all the major constituencies of umbrage — the self-appointed, unofficial watch committees for ever on the lookout for some injudicious turn of phrase or unguarded sentence that can lead to accusations of sexism, chauvinism, racism or homophobic bias.

On top of the usual current areas of social sensitivity there are the myriad stipulations of the law and fast-proliferating codes of practice. These are likely to circumscribe severely the terms in which, for example, financial services and health products are described. In many countries, data protection legislation regulates the use which marketers can make of information that they gather about their customers. There is also a plethora of codes whose stipulations have been framed to outlaw the use of unsubstantiable and misleading claims.

These codes of practice have multiplied alarmingly. In the UK alone, conscientious and nervous copywriters will have on their bookshelves beside the usual dictionary and thesaurus the following: The Code of Practice of the Direct Marketing Association; The British Codes of Advertising and Sales Promotion; the Code Issued by the Data Protection Registrar; The Code of Advertising Practice of the Advertising Standards Authority; the Green Claims Code (which is designed to regulate claims concerning practices that are said to be environmentally friendly); and Notes of Guidance for Broadcasters and Advertisers issued by the Broadcast Advertising Clearance Centre. Any time left over after studying these with the diligent attention that their draughtsmen no doubt envisaged is presumably available for creative work!

The enormous proliferation of well-intentioned codes of practice — the insatiable zeal for self-regulation, presumably as an alternative to regulations imposed by government — has had one paradoxical effect. The sheer number, length and complexity of these codes has made it virtually impossible for any interested party to gain more than a smattering of knowledge of their stipulations. As a result, the influence and value of these documents — far from increasing — is probably declining.

For the concerned direct marketer therefore, the sensible policy boils down to a simple set of rules: refrain from misleading or unsubstantiable claims; try not to offend the susceptibilities of normal, reasonable people; do not exploit people's fears of injury or illness; take the trouble to learn the more important rules of trade associations of which your organisation is a member; take as much trouble to win the respect and liking of your readers as you would to secure the same reactions from those whom you encounter in person.

Appendix 2

Practice Exercises

While I hope that the advice and suggestions contained in this book will prove useful to readers, it occurs to me that some might find it helpful to be offered an opportunity to put into practice immediately the principles explained without waiting to be given their next professional assignment.

So here are some creative writing exercises that provide you with a chance to tackle the challenge of writing copy for some fairly typical assignments. Their purpose is simply to enable you to exercise your copywriting "muscles" and get the creative juices flowing.

Afterwards, you might find it useful to look at what you have written in the light of the techniques and principles described in the appropriate chapters. Try to be honest and ruthlessly self-critical, and refrain (as any client or prospective customer would be bound to do) from giving what you have written the benefit of any doubt. Good luck!

Motivation Analysis (Chapter 1)

- List as many motivations as you can think of for buying a camera.

Creative Levers (Chapter 3)

- Think up ways of using the various creative levers described in Chapter 3 (Promise, Change, Challenge etc) to sell the *Oxford English Dictionary* and the *Times Atlas of the World*.

Writing Letters (Chapter 4)

- As winter approaches a garage proposes to write to customers offering — at a special price — a pre-winter car "health check" (of tyres, lights, brakes etc) and a range of seasonal accessories such as snow-tyres, chains and headlamps. Write an appropriate personalised letter.

- Write an appropriate letter from a firm of travel agents to send to a customer who is known to be interested in wildlife, designed to persuade him to come in and see what is on offer this year.

- Write a letter inviting readers who are presumed to be comfortably off to become customers of Barclays Bank.

- Draft a letter that makes a good case for taking out buildings insurance with Sun Alliance & Royal.

- Write a letter designed to persuade a self-employed reader to take out a pension policy with a mutual insurance company (such as Equitable Life) that does not have to pay dividends to shareholders.

- A chain of supermarkets has announced a new loyalty card that entitles holders to such benefits as discounts and free gifts. Write a letter that will be sent, along with the card, to customers who apply.

Brochures (Chapter 5)

- Write the main headlines for a brochure designed to sell the *Times Atlas of the World*.

- What creative building blocks can you come up with for a brochure that promotes the *A-Z Gardener's Encyclopaedia Of Plants And Flowers* published by the Royal Horticultural Society?

- How many creative building blocks can you devise for a letter and brochure designed to sell a subscription to the Consumers' Association Magazine, *Which*?

- Now choose from these building blocks those which might make an effective brochure and arrange these, with headlines and captions, in a suitable sequence to create the framework of a good brochure.

Press Ads (Chapter 5)

- Write a whole-page advertisement to appear in the magazine at Christmas time inviting *Good Housekeeping* readers and subscribers to give subscriptions to friends and relatives as gifts. Those who do so will be given a 20 per cent discount on the regular price and will receive an unspecified "Christmas present".

- Write a press ad for a space that measures 8" across three columns in one of the quality dailies inviting readers to send for a free booklet that describes an insurance policy that provides cover against the risk of being made redundant.

Sweepstakes and Contests (Chapter 7)

- Write a letter of up to 300 words that offers the reader — in return for replying to your offer — a chance to win one of 500 cash prizes (of which the biggest is £100,000) in a post-drawn sweepstakes.

- Now make the same offer for a pre-draw.

- Write a letter that invites the holder of a household insurance policy to increase the value of the cover it provides.

- Now add, as an incentive to do so, the offer of a chance to win in a contest (open only to policyholders) a £25,000 prestige car.

Business To Business Selling (Chapter 8)

- A company which markets beverage vending machines asks you to write a letter to managing directors of companies that are known not to have such a machine, making the case for installing them and suggesting an appointment for a demonstration.

- An employment agency that specialises in legal staff wants a letter promoting its services that it can send to a list of solicitors.

Handling Complaints and Getting Bills Paid (Chapter 9)

- Draft a suitable reply to a complaint from a customer who has bought a domestic appliance (freezer or refrigerator) that proved defective within three weeks of purchase.

- Reply to a customer who has complained about the accommodation in a Majorcan hotel which he chose for a family holiday. Although he complains that his holiday was ruined, the tour operator is not prepared to refund more than £100.

- Write a letter demanding long-overdue payment from a garage customer who has not paid a repair and service bill for £250.

- Try your hand at a suitable letter to accompany the sixth and final bill in a series seeking payment for a subscription to an up-market magazine such as *Country Life*.

Retention, Renewal and Regeneration (Chapter 10)

- Write a letter that American Express can send to former holders of the card who have allowed their membership to lapse, inviting them to rejoin.

- Write a letter that the AA can send those who have allowed membership to lapse, inviting them to reapply for membership.

How to Raise Funds for Charity (Chapter 11)

- Since the cost cannot be met from the NHS budget, a group of residents plans to raise enough money to buy a CAT Scanner for the local hospital. It falls to you to write a letter that will go to all households in the area asking for donations to the scanner appeal.

- The Royal Society for the Protection of Birds wishes to buy a stretch of Suffolk coastline in order to create a reserve for sea birds, including a number of rare and threatened species. You are asked to write a letter that the RSPB can mail to all its members appealing for contributions to the fund set up to finance the purchase. The sum needed is £1 million and a rich philanthropist has agreed to match whatever sum is raised by members.

Political Persuasion (Chapter 12)

- The Liberal Democrats plan a recruitment drive. Write a letter (to be signed by the Leader) that invites readers to join the Party.

Appendix 3

Creative Checklist

Before a word of copy is written, you might find it helpful to run through this checklist, either in your own mind or with the copywriter. (This is not an encouragement to make a six-course banquet out of a ham sandwich, so I would recommend that you use only such elements of this checklist as seem appropriate to the nature of your offer — and, above all, useful and relevant to *you*. At the end of the day, you are not trying to land a spacecraft, the checklist is advisory not mandatory!)

Motivation

General

- Why might anyone want a product or service of this nature — what needs will it meet, what uses has it, what functions will it perform?

Specific

- What are the most significant features of the product or service?

- What unique, exclusive or distinctive features does it have?

- In what respects, if any, is it arguably superior to the competition?

Market

- Who might be persuaded to spend money on it?

- Would they be buying it for their own use, or primarily for others?

- What kind of people are they likely to be?

- What sort of problems do they face?

- To what credible situations is it relevant?

Offer

- Do the terms on which the product is offered include any special incentives — discount, premium (free gift), chances to win in a sweepstakes or contest?

- How much emphasis does it make sense to give them?

Copy Approaches

Which of these copy levers or approaches can you realistically expect to make use of?

❑ Change

❑ Challenge

❑ Promise

❑ Empowerment

❑ Evocation

❑ Categories

- ☐ Opposites

- ☐ Flattery

- ☐ Novelty.

What emotions come into the picture?

- ☐ Nostalgia

- ☐ Ambition

- ☐ Vanity

- ☐ Pride

- ☐ Anxiety

- ☐ Cupidity

- ☐ Fear

- ☐ Protectiveness

- ☐ Impatience

- ☐ Idleness.

Or, in the case of a charity appeal:

- ☐ Pity

- ☐ Anger

- ☐ Sympathy

- ☐ Concern

- ☐ Idealism.

Medium

How is the offer to be made:

☐ Press Ad

☐ Mailing Package

☐ Catalogue

☐ TV

☐ Radio

☐ Internet.

Type of Response

☐ Mail

☐ Telephone

☐ Fax

☐ E-mail

Package

What are to be the components of the mailing package:

☐ Letter

☐ Brochure

☐ Catalogue

☐ Order Form

Index